Children at risk?

Safety as a social value

Helen Roberts
Susan J. Smith
Carol Bryce

Open University Press
Buckingham · Philadelphia

Open University Press
Celtic Court
22 Ballmoor
Buckingham
MK18 1XW

and
1900 Frost Road, Suite 101
Bristol, PA 19007, USA

First Published 1995

A catalogue record of this book is available from the British Library

ISBN   0 335 19210 6 (pb)

Library of Congress Cataloging-in-Publication Data
Roberts, Helen, 1949–
    Children at risk? : safety as a social value / by Helen Roberts,
Susan J. Smith, Carol Bryce.
        p.   cm.
    Includes bibliographical references and index.
    ISBN 0–335–19210–6 (pbk.)
    1. Children's accidents—Great Britain—Sociological aspects.
2. Children's accidents. I. Smith, Susan J., 1956– . II. Bryce,
Carol, 1963– . III. Title.
HV675.72.R6 1995
363.1'083—dc20   95–9567
                                                                      CIP

Typeset by Dorwyn Ltd, Rowlands Castle, Hants
Printed in Great Britain by St Edmundsbury Press Ltd,
Bury St Edmunds, Suffolk

Contents

Acknowledgements

Our greatest debt in writing this book, and carrying out the work on which it is based, is owed to the people of Corkerhill who first invited us into their community and then participated so wholeheartedly in this project. As we describe in the first chapter, Betty Campbell, Walter Morrison and Cathie Rice were pivotal to the success of the work. But many other people in the community contributed to the design an implementation of the project. Some time after the research was completed, the city council agreed to spend £950,000 on central heating for 346 flat-roofed homes in the area. Cathie Rice wrote at the time:

> I feel strongly that this level of investment is achieved by the efforts of the many people who have been involved from the Damphouse enquiry to the WHO Safe Communities status, including, of course, the child accident research. I have no doubt that every tenant who took part in the research, or attended meetings or filled in local questionnaires feel that they have contributed to this, and rightly so.

The empirical work described in the book was carried out while Helen Roberts and Carol Bryce were employed by the University of Glasgow. A number of colleagues there were very helpful to us at various stages of the research process. These include Rita Dobbs, Philip McLoone, Alastair Leyland and David Stone. Our part-time secretary Margaret Reilly was an outstanding asset to the project, and is surely the best data coder in the West of Scotland. Michelle Lloyd was research assistant for the group interviews described in this book, and this preliminary work was supported by a small grant from the Trustees of the Nuffield Foundation, to whom we are most grateful. The project would not have got off the ground without it. The empirical work for the main study was funded by the Chief Scientist Office of the Scottish Office Home and Health Department through an addition to the core funding of the Public Health Research Unit of the University of Glasgow. We valued this funding and the constructive criticism and advice of Dr Anne Ruckley in the Chief Scientist Office.

In carrying out this work, we were also greatly assisted by our colleagues in the Medical Research Council's Medical Sociology Unit in Glasgow. A number of the questions we asked had been used in their 2007 study, and two-thirds of our interviewers were recruited via the MRC unit. Barbara Jamieson, the survey manager at the MRC, was always helpful to us, and provided assistance with the interviewer training. Our excellent interviewers were Edith Hamilton and Sheena Mitchell (who also carried out the in-depth case studies described in this book), Sylvia Black, Janet Crossan, Anne Grant, Morag Graydon, Theresa McElhone and Jean McPhee. The unusually high response rates reported in this book (95 per cent of all families in Corkerhill with children aged 14 and under agreed to be interviewed) are owing to both the skills of our interviewers and the commitment of the community to the research. Members of the Health Promotion Department of the Greater Glasgow Health Board discussed aspects of the work with us, and we are grateful to all the service professionals who assisted us formally or informally with this work.

We are grateful to the Child Accident Prevention Trust for permission to use figure 1.2, and to the authors of *Children, Teenagers and Health: The Key Data* (Woodroffe *et al.*, Open University Press, 1993) whose figures drawn from OPCS data we have used for figures 1.1 and 1.3.

Barry Pless, at the time of our work a visiting fellow at the Child Accident Prevention Trust, and Michael Hayes from the Child Accident Prevention Trust both gave us useful advice on the collection of data on accident events.

After we completed the study, but before we completed the book, a number of other people helped us in various ways. They include Hilda Mankin, Joan Pickton and David Potter at Barnardos; Sue Maclachlan at the University of Edinburgh, who checked and typed the references and Sylvia Potter who compiled our index. As ever, books are greedy of time and space, and our families have been helpful to us in a variety of ways in enabling the project to be completed.

Safety as a social value, our sub-title, is a phrase used by William Haddon, Edward Suchman and David Klein in the introduction to their important book on accident research (Haddon *et al.*, 1964). Although we use the phrase in a rather different sense, we are grateful to these authors for a focus which guided some of our work in the planning stage.

Finally, our editor at Open University Press, Jacinta Evans, and her colleague Joan Malherbe have been supportive and helpful at every stage, despite delays on our part. Claire Hutchins, our desk editor and John Taylor our copy-editor, ensured a smooth passage for the book. However, the book is dedicated to the people living in Corkerhill, who continue to live with the problems we describe.

Helen Roberts
Susan J. Smith
Carol Bryce

Edinburgh and London

List of figures and tables

Figures

Tables

1

Introduction

Children and society

Children, it is still widely assumed, should be seen and not heard. As a consequence much social science, like much public policy, fails to recognize that even in the 'ageing' societies of North-western Europe people aged 14 and under account for as much as 20 per cent of the population (Jensen and Saporiti 1992). Of course, there are specialist branches in a number of disciplines which are explicitly concerned with children's circumstances and problems – child psychology, paediatrics and so on. And there are special areas of public policy devoted to children's concerns – the child abuse machinery, the primary and secondary education systems and other essential children's services. But within the mainstream of social science and the mainstream of policy-making, children are often marginal or absent altogether. They don't vote, they aren't a feature of the social contract, they don't make money and, as far as the public arena is concerned, it has seemed until recently that they don't much matter.

The picture of neglect has begun to change, partly as a consequence of the emotive publicity around child abuse issues, partly as a consequence of the position of children in the human rights movement and partly as intellectual fashions have changed in a direction that favours research on children's affairs. Nevertheless, the majority of published work still focuses on child abuse, child development and child-rearing, even though children's social life, their subjection to social control and their social geographies are quite different from those of the adult world. Most importantly for our purposes, of course, childhood is also a uniquely dangerous time of life.

Perinatal and infant mortality have fallen dramatically in the Western world. This is a key feature of the so-called epidemiological transition through which most countries of the economically developed world have passed. The odds of a child in the UK surviving the hazards of birth and avoiding death from a major infectious disease are higher now than they have ever been. However, we all know that our children are still at risk from a variety of hazards: not those caused by micro-organisms and viruses, but rather those inherent in the lifestyles, environments and social mores of the modern world.

From the publicity surrounding child protection, we might assume that the biggest risk comes from abuse at home by a member of the family; on the other hand, from the attentions drawn to 'stranger danger' and the dramatic media coverage of recent child murders, the threat posed by outsiders might seem more immediate. Then again, the campaigns of the major health charities show that continuing susceptibility to cancer or leukaemia is another crucial compromise to children's well-being.

All these risks are real. Yet, in practice, the biggest threat to children in Britain is nowhere near so obvious or so widely publicized. It is the prospect of death or disability resulting from accidental injury in the home or on the streets. Ironically, while libraries and bookshops are well provided with work on child abuse, much of it excellent, books on children's accidents would not fill even a short shelf. This volume is, in part, an attempt to redress the imbalance.

Childhood accidents

Accidents are by far the most important single cause of death in childhood in Western countries. Figure 1.1 indicates that almost half of all deaths among children aged 1–19 in the United Kingdom in 1990 were due to injury and poisoning. It has been estimated that children's accidents result annually in 700 fatalities, 120,000 hospital admissions and about two million casualty department attendances in England and Wales alone (Child Accident Prevention Trust (CAPT) 1989). The cost in financial terms to the National Health Service, the fire service, the police, the ambulance service, insurers and others is often unmeasured, though the financial outlay made by the NHS may be as high as £1 million per district per year (1991 prices) (CAPT 1992). The total annual cost of child accidents to the health service sector has been estimated to run to £200 million (Stone 1993). The additional toll of these accidents in social and emotional terms on children, parents and other carers is immeasurable, as are the effects of anxiety on children and adults who are faced every day with risky situations in which, to use the imagery of Hillman *et al.* (1990), one false move may result in injury or death.

Although deaths by accident have made a contribution to the mortality transition and have fallen by a quarter over the past half century, this

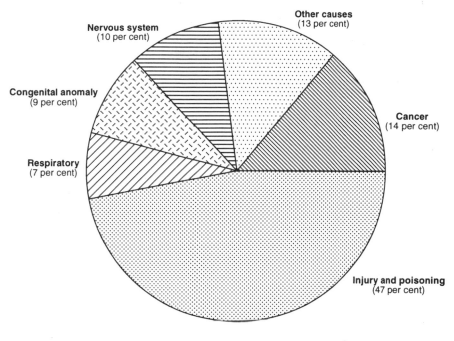

Total 4488 deaths

Figure 1.1   Main causes of death in the UK for people aged 1 to 19, in 1990.
Source: OPCS and Registrar General for Scotland and Northern Ireland after Woodroffe *et al.* (1993).

decline has not been anything like as significant as the decline in deaths from other causes. This is clear from Figure 1.2. As a consequence, injuries, including accidental injuries, are responsible for a growing proportion of deaths among children and young adults (Woodroffe *et al.* 1993). Despite this, our understanding of the aetiology of child accidents is poor, largely because the available sources of official data provide an inadequate basis for understanding the social distribution of accidents. What we do know may be summarized as follows.

For children under the age of five, accidents are most likely to take place in the home (where toddlers spend most of their time). After the age of five, accidents outside the home, and particularly on the roads, are more common. Scotland, where the work that forms the case study for this book was carried out, has (together with Northern Ireland) a worse accident rate for children than the rest of the United Kingdom, and the UK in turn has an unenviable record in relation to other European countries. Figure 1.3 shows the dismal ranking of the UK in terms of child pedestrian deaths. In the UK,

Rate per million living

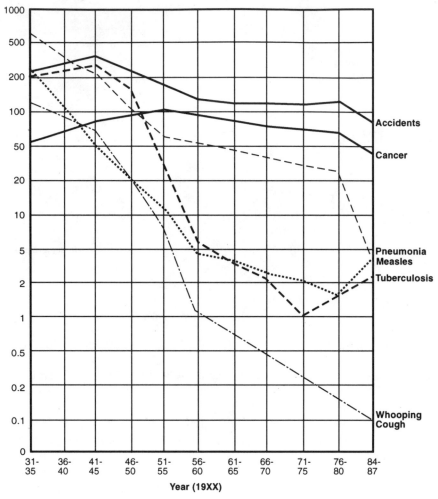

Figure 1.2 Mortality rates from selected causes for children aged 1 to 14, England and Wales, 1931–1987.
Source: OPCS, Deaths by cause, *Quarterly Monitor* DH2 88/3 (1988), after CAPT (1989).

one child in 15 is injured in a road accident before his or her sixteenth birthday (Jones 1990). For children under ten the death rate is three times higher in the UK than in Sweden. For 10–14-year-olds, Britain's child pedestrian death rate is one of the worst in Europe (Avery and Jackson 1993).

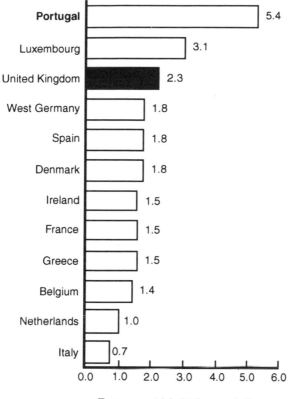

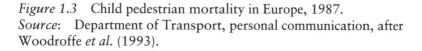

Rate per 100,000 population

Figure 1.3   Child pedestrian mortality in Europe, 1987.
Source: Department of Transport, personal communication, after
Woodroffe *et al.* (1993).

Not only is the overall child accident rate in the UK alarmingly high, it is
coupled with a striking social class gradient in accident events. As Kenneth
Macdonald (1995) observes,

> An impending child, engaged in a quasi-Rawlsian assessment of coun-
> tries as potential places to be born into, and fretting about the risk of
> violent early death, might view the variations in accidental death rates
> as swamping the relatively trivial divergence in homicides.

In the UK the steep social class gradient in accidents has frequently been
observed, and it is more marked than the gradient associated with any other
health inequality, yet it remains poorly explained. It also goes hand in hand
with a substantial imbalance between the sexes (boys are significantly more

likely to have an accident and to be killed in an accident than are girls) and with enduring spatial variations in accident-proneness (those living in poor neighbourhoods face greater risks than their counterparts in higher income areas) (Backett and Johnson 1959; Alwash and McCarthy 1988a, b; Pharaoh and Alberman 1990).

The social class gradient for childhood accidents deserves special mention because it is steeper than the class gradient for all other causes of death (Townsend *et al.* 1988; Avery *et al.* 1990). Children aged 0–14 with fathers in social class V are twice as likely to die from any cause as their counterparts born to fathers in social class I. However, such children are three times more likely to die from an accident and five times more likely to die by being hit by a car; and the gap between classes for deaths caused by fires, falls and drowning is even higher (Kendrick 1994). These class differences in accident-related mortality are greatest in 1–4-year-olds and for boys. In this age group, the mortality ratios between social classes V and I are 3.38 for boys and 2.58 for girls. The figures for 5–9-year-olds are 2.07 for boys and 1.85 for girls, and the ratios for 10–14-year-olds are 1.77 and 1.58 respectively (Pharaoh and Alberman 1990).

Income level variations in child mortality of this order are particularly marked in Britain (Sunderland 1984; Constantinides and Walker 1986; Avery *et al.* 1990; Avery and Jackson 1993), although they have been found in other developed countries, such as the United States (Wise *et al.* 1985) and Canada (Dougherty *et al.* 1990). However, there are many societies – notably the other welfare state countries of Europe – where risk inequalities are much less notable. It is unlikely that the British observations are artefactual, not least because the imbalance in risks is apparent in both mortality and morbidity data. While the latter may be difficult to interpret, and to compare between one health authority or health board and another, the same is not true of mortality data. There are no inter-hospital variations in the diagnosis of death. A dead child is a dead child; the inequality in child mortality resulting from accidents is a social fact in Britain.

The steep social gradients in child accident risk were quantified over 15 years ago by those preparing the Black Report, and the inequalities they signalled were targeted as important issues for action and investigation (Working Group on Inequalities in Health 1980). Yet in the years that followed neither politicians nor researchers paid much attention to the problem. Thus, although legislation recently introduced as part of the restructuring of the health and welfare sector does target accidents as an issue for attention, it mentions neither risky environments nor health inequalities as policy relevant affairs. Much of the academic literature also evades the inequalities debate by focusing on the behavioural, cultural, familial and maternal factors that predispose children to accidents. Brown and Davidson (1978), for instance, found maternal depression to be an indicator of risk, events leading up to, surrounding and occurring in the aftermath of accidents. The range of individual accident and near-accident 'case studies' as well as the various collective views on accident risks are drawn on throughout the book, but the methodology is discussed more fully in Chapter 2. The individual and group interviews we conducted draw on the 'story-telling' tradition so well described by Hilary Graham (1983, 1984a). The narrative, or the story, the 'what happened next and what then happened', was, we felt, a particularly appropriate way of gathering information about accidents. As Graham has pointed out, story-telling allows some redress of the power balance in social research. It allows the informant to control the flow and content of information imparted. Story-telling counters the tendency other ways of information gathering may have of fracturing experiences. The 'injury event' can be put in the context of what else was going on, of how people felt at the time and afterwards. The emphasis is on telling rather than 'responding'.

Finally, using the strategies outlined above we attempt to *develop methods of monitoring accidents and risks which are as sensitive to parents' as to professionals' views* of the causes and consequences of accidents. A number of studies, including our own, suggest that parents' levels of awareness of accidents to children in general, and of specific risks, is high (Colver *et al.* 1982; Roberts *et al.* 1993). Although the environmental, social and behavioural factors involved are well documented – if still inadequately understood – through a series of longitudinal studies (e.g. Bijur *et al.* 1988a; Pless *et al.* 1989), what is neither adequately documented nor properly explained is how most parents manage to maintain their children in safety most of the time. Even in a high risk area, safety is the dominant social value. Yet we seem far less interested in how people succeed in keeping children safe than in the relatively few occasions on which safe-keeping strategies fail. As a consequence, little is known about the ways in which a desire to maintain child safety is incorporated into the routine behaviours which structure daily life. Our study is designed in part to provide some general information on this neglected theme.

In addition to collecting epidemiological data on accidents, near accidents and perceived risks, therefore, we also investigated (through qualitative and quantitative methods) what children and parents who live in a hazardous environment know about safety and risk, and we assessed where this knowledge lies in people's priorities for organizing their lives. How do people use the information they have about risk, and what are the barriers to using it more effectively?

Our main point in documenting accidents, risks and reactions is to argue that while the risk to an individual may be difficult to calculate, and while there is an element of unpredictability in whether a given set of circumstances will lead to an accident, and in whether that accident will lead to

injury or death, the distribution of accidents is something all too predictable. Accidents may appear to happen at random, but accident events are
not randomly distributed. They may appear to be unavoidable, but in the
course of this book we argue that many accidents are both predictable and
preventable. Furthermore, the challenge, if this is true, is not simply to
recognize that risk is patterned, but rather to define and discriminate between risks that are 'acceptable' (part of the living of life in the late twen-
tieth century) and those that can't be tolerated (and that result from and
contribute to a series of social inequalities that undermine people's rights
and entitlements). The challenge is to identify risks that could not be reduced without compromising some much valued aspects of twentieth-
century life, and risks that signal the kind of inequalities that could and
should be ameliorated. It is our contention that these risks can be defined
and assessed and that, in the interests of child safety, this should be a
research priority.

Whose responsibility?

Our first argument in this book is that child accidents cannot justly be
ignored or marginalized on the grounds that they defy prediction or control.
Our second argument explores, and in the end challenges, the idea that if the
problem is policy-worthy, then these policies should be primarily about risk
awareness and education. We seek to resist the idea embedded in so much
legislation and professional practice that responsibility for prevention lies
solely, or even primarily, with parents and individuals rather than with the
community or the state. Furthermore, our findings question the view that if
the state has a role it is primarily to tell parents things they are assumed not
to know about accident risks.

A second reason why there has been so little public and political engage-
ment with the challenge posed by childhood accidents is the success with
which collective responsibilities for risky environments and activities have
been displaced on to individual parents, especially mothers, and children.
This tendency characterizes virtually the whole history of interventions in
children's lives, and it now pervades a wide range of public health policies
(Tesh 1988). So it was that when accidents began to emerge as a new and
serious threat to child health at the turn of the century (Zelizer 1986),
'proper' mothering was quickly identified as an important arena for action
and intervention. Although safety efforts were sometimes promoted and
financed by tram companies, while police initiated safety training for school
teachers and children were organized into junior safety councils, a strong
undercurrent was that 'if these little ones are to be saved, it is the mothers
. . . that must save them' (Tarbell 1922, quoted in Zelizer 1986). Through
public campaigns, therefore, responsibility for managing accidents was

Pless *et al.* (1989) found overcrowding and family problems to be import-ant, and Wadsworth *et al.* (1983) found associations between accident rates and single-parent families, step-parents, frequent household moves, low maternal age and perceived poor behaviour in the child.

From a sociological point of view, therefore, child accidents in general, and risk inequalities in particular, continue to present a challenge. In the years since the Black Report was published, little has changed in the overall picture of child accidents, and accidental death still has the steepest social class gradient of all causes of death in childhood. So, while accidents ac-count for a large proportion of child deaths, they are not randomly dis-tributed and their magnitude and patterning are only poorly understood. Some of the epidemiological literature charting the distribution of child accident deaths and major morbidity does provide a starting point for an understanding of accidents as socially patterned events (e.g. Blondel *et al.* 1985; Avery *et al.* 1990). And a few studies are beginning to confront the inequality problem, notably the work of Constantinides and Walker (1986) on child accidents and inequality in a London borough and, more recently, the report by the North West Regional Health Authority on reducing death and injury in children (Popay and Young 1993). However, much remains to be done.

In an attempt to fill in some gaps in the documentation and explanation of child accident risk, this book explores the problem of children's accidents from a sociological and geographical perspective. We begin, in the remainder of this introduction, by thinking about the reasons why child accidents have hitherto had such low priority in the academic, social services and political agenda. We want to understand why it is that the equivalent of three under-fives can die in accidents every week without it becoming a major national cause for concern. We argue that the answer has something to do with how accidents are conceived of, monitored and constructed as a policy issue.

We then go on, in the core of the book, to draw on a series of case study materials to explore some of the ways in which it may be possible to change the prevailing agenda. We begin with the premiss that neither a high overall accident rate nor a steep socio-economic gradient is inevitable; and we show how both these social problems may be tackled, first by finding effective ways to measure and monitor the antecedents, incidence and effects of the accidents themselves and, second, by recognizing that local knowledge can provide the basis of effective prevention policies.

A neglected problem

Given the sheer extent of the child accident problem it is at best curious – at worst scandalous – that accident risks have not given rise to the same public concern that other aspects of children's well-being have elicited. Where, when we look at accidents, are the public enquiries and the child protection infrastructure that we associate with the threat of child abuse? Why do accidents, which are relatively common yet often very serious events, have such a low profile when compared to other threats to child well-being? Why are the more exotic problems faced by children, such as satanic abuse, so much more newsworthy and so much more likely to attract the attention of researchers and funders than events which inflict similar amounts of suffering but are classified as 'accidents'? Why do we remove children from 'dangerous families' but tolerate 'dangerous places'? Why do 'disasters' involving multiple deaths at a single, rare, moment attract so much more attention than the same number of deaths that occur much more frequently from a series of 'one-off' events? Why is it that the major cause of childhood death in the United Kingdom does not attract more attention from scholars, policy-makers and the public?

Part of the answer is that politicians and policy-makers have defined accident risks in ways that allow society to avoid or evade the problem. Accidents are the only major cause of morbidity and mortality readily described by professionals as well as lay people in extra-rational terms. 'Tragic, but unavoidable' is how child accidents are often described. Concepts such as 'bad luck' and 'acts of God' have remained culturally acceptable as 'explanations' for accidents throughout a period of rationalization and modernization in the conceptualization of other kinds of risk (Haddon *et al.* 1964). Some children are mysteriously thought to be more 'accident prone' than others, even though there is little empirical evidence to support this idea. As a consequence, the public and policy-makers alike tend to assume that accidents cannot accurately be measured, monitored or anticipated, and that the best we can do to prevent them is to ensure that parents and children are educated sufficiently to recognize the risks.

The problem of child accidents has thus been marginalized in the policy arena to the extent that thoughts of having to tackle the problem have, until recently, been avoided. Why should this be? We think that there are two main reasons. First, it is generally assumed that children's accidents are unique, individual, unpredictable and idiosyncratic. If accidents are portrayed in this way, it follows that there is no rational basis for intervening in them in a systematic way. Second, if this first assertion is true, then the best we can hope for is that parents will take care. In so far as any kind of prevention is possible it can best be achieved through the exhortation and education of individuals. Our aim in what follows is to explore the origins and validity of these ideas. Is the marginalization of child accidents a logical consequence of the nature of child accidents, or is it a politically convenient way of evading a crucial social issue?

Assessing the risks

It is tempting to think not only that the problems of securing usable accident data far outweigh the gains to be made from new policy directions, but that child accidents are so random and unpredictable that even the most precise data-set would be of limited value in predicting, and thus controlling, future accident events. Accordingly, while there are a number of distinct bodies of literature on the risks faced by children, on child accidents, on risk management and on child safety, there are many aspects of the incidence, distribution and effects of accidents that are unknown and unstudied. Those which are studied, moreover, tend to be based on a rather narrow body of evidence.

Accidents are unusual in social research in that most of the work touching on this subject is not about 'accidents' at all, but about their injury-producing effects. Thus, although there are a number of sources of official data on child accidents, the information produced is all about injuries and their causes. This means that the medical model is the one most widely applied in accident studies and this has influenced the sorts of research questions asked. Crudely conceived, accidents have a single cause and a single effect, and the former is defined and recognized with reference to the latter. Thus, mortality data are seen as the most dependable of the accident statistics (though even these rely on accurate coding of the cause of death), while figures on accidents resulting in hospital admissions, which can be obtained from patient discharge forms, are a further common indicator of accident risk. For example, in 1993 there were 2,686 females and 4,047 males (per 100,000 population) aged 14 and under discharged from hospital in Scotland following a diagnosis of injuries or poisoning (Information and Statistics Division 1994).

These figures look convincing enough but they do not provide a count of children treated and discharged on the same day, or of those treated in accident and emergency departments. This kind of information can currently only be estimated on the basis of the Home and Leisure Accident Surveillance Scheme systems (HASS and LASS), which survey 18 and 13 hospitals respectively and collect data on accidents that prompted accident and emergency department visits. (HASS was originally set up in 1976 and surveyed hospitals in England and Wales. In 1988 coverage was extended to 22 hospitals, including Scotland and Northern Ireland, giving UK-wide coverage. Then in 1990 the number of hospitals in the survey was reduced to 18 following refinement of the system of data collection.) While these data (on where, when and how accidents happened, their outcomes and associated injuries) are believed to be reliable, there are some doubts about the wisdom of extrapolating them to the UK as a whole. (The latest figures, for 1993, show 626,000 home accidents to males and 497,000 home accidents to females aged 14 and under, and 868,000 males and 528,000 females aged 14 or under were involved in leisure accidents (Consumer Safety Unit 1995).) Additionally, while work associated with the Home and Leisure Accidents Surveillance Scheme has been influential in identifying and modifying some specific hazards, the data again concentrate on the existence and extent of the injury – on the *consequences* of the accident, rather than on the causes and circumstances of the unplanned events that, on this occasion, led to the injury. Moreover, the number of individuals treated by their general practitioner following an accident are not collected through the HASS and LASS systems and data on the number and types of injuries treated by doctors are not readily available. But even if they were, they would be of the same type as the information already discussed – they would be concerned with the medical consequences of an accident event.

In short, the main official sources of data on the character and incidence of child accidents provide only a partial description of the aetiology of accident events. They refer only to accidents which lead to injuries, and for the most part they refer only to injuries treated in particular kinds of health service outlet. Ironically, accidents at home are the worst documented of all. Currently, home accidents are not notifiable (in contrast to accidents at work) and they go largely unrecorded. While accidents at work have to be recorded in an accident book and reported to the relevant authorities, home accidents do not normally have to be so fully accounted for. Likewise, accidents to children in their 'workplaces' – the schools – tend to be recorded only for routine administrative purposes (e.g. insurance claims) unless they are very serious (when the Health and Safety Executive has to be informed).

The official data thus underestimate the true incidence of accidents, leaving a hidden figure of unreported and unrecorded events – both injury-producing and others – whose character may be important when designing prevention strategies. Not only are official statistics a gross underestimate, but it is also unlikely that the selected accident events that they contain are in any way typical or representative of all accident events. They may represent the events that people think of as most serious, since accidents which do not prompt a visit to the statutory health services are generally thought of as more minor and therefore less important than accidents which result in potentially severe injury. And, of course, if the cost of accidents is measured in terms of health service expenditure this kind of figure is important.

We can say nothing reliable about causes and prevention of accidents from injury data, however. We do not know whether the antecedents of events which lead to serious injury are, or are not, similar to those of accident events which never cause injury, or lead only to minor falls and bruises. For instance, a child putting a knitting needle into an unprotected electric socket may be electrocuted and die, thus ensuring a place in medical statistics as an accidental death. She may be badly burned, and become an assigned to the family and this formed the focus for child safety crusades. Since then, children have been increasingly domesticated, supervised and confined (Donzelot 1979), and the 'problem' of dealing with child safety has conveniently been shifted from the public to the private domain (Roberts and Coggan 1994).

Today, the starting point of a great deal of British (and other) work on child accidents remains rooted in the idea that children are a danger to themselves, and that parents are deficient in their safe-keeping activities. Accidents happen, according to this line of reasoning, because children and their parents are not well enough informed, are not properly competent or do not have the right safety equipment (Kendrick 1994). The poor performance of mothers and children can be modified by health visitors, health promoters or road safety officers, but the direction of information on safety and accidents is very clearly top down. In contrast, the ultimate responsibility for children's well-being is quite definitely bottom-up. Accident prevention is not big business in the world of public policy because it is a duty discharged by parents, not a sphere of intervention by the state.

This stress on the safe-keeping responsibilities of victims is both expressed in, and explained by, the influential literature relating to accident prevention and health promotion. The truism that prevention is better than cure has a number of attractions. 'Cure' or intervention in the face of ill health can be costly both for individuals and for the health services. The fact that prevention can be cheap (or even free) makes it an attractive option for health service providers. It is also attractive to politicians. As Stone (1989: 1) has pointed out, 'health education is cheap, generally uncontroversial and safe: if it works, politicians take the credit, and if it does not, the target population takes the blame.' Thus major campaigns have been launched to suggest that by changing our unhealthy behaviour, diet and smoking habits, we can alter our risk of premature death from coronary heart disease and lung cancer in the desired direction. Prevention as a way of avoiding unpleasant and untimely death thus occupies a high moral ground, although the evidence that behaviour has a substantial effect on public health when compared with other causal factors is slim (Roberts and Coggan 1994).

As the leading cause of death to children after the age of one in the United Kingdom and elsewhere in the developed world, child accidents are, predictably enough, a significant focus of preventive activity of the type outlined above. A number of targets have been set for accident reduction including a World Health Organization (WHO) target of a reduction in accidents of all types by at least 25 per cent by the year 2000 from a 1980 baseline, and a Department of Transport target for a reduction in road casualties in Great Britain of one-third by the year 2000 from a baseline of average casualties from 1981 to 1985. The target set by the government in *The Health of the Nation* in relation to child deaths is a reduction in the death rate for accidents to under-15s in England and Wales by at least 33 per cent by 2005. The White Paper that set this target signalled, though, that the government intended to rely primarily on information and education for the prevention of accidents 'and to avoid the imposition of unnecessary regulations on business and individuals' (HMSO 1992: 106). In Scotland, meanwhile, there is no national target, and there is an expectation that figures will be set locally. The powerful child protection machinery which grinds into action when child abuse is suspected – and there are detailed regulations which set out the procedures for the protection of children (DoH 1988, 1991) – does not operate in any useful way in protecting children from hazardous environments. And while, technically, a child can be removed from a home or a dwelling because of dangerous or 'accidentogenic' features, we do not find roads being closed down because they represent a consistent danger to children, or schools closed because there are no smoke alarms.

Cooper's (1993) work gives some clues as to why this is. Child abuse cases, unlike child accidents, have become social symbols: 'they make a statement about something going wrong in society' (Cooper 1993: 7). Society, accordingly, makes an effort to put it right. The only time child accidents perform this social function is when a large number of deaths occurs in a single event, such as on a school outing. For this and other reasons, there is no public outcry about the dangers that every child, even the most privileged, has to negotiate every day of her or his life when crossing the road. Rather, when accident risks are tackled it is the child or parent (usually the mother) who is seen as the problem.

'Dangerousness' is a quality more likely to be attributed to people than to places (Parton 1985, 1991), and whereas policies on child abuse are predicated on the assumption that the child is innocent, there is a very strongly child-blaming or child-responsible culture in relation to child accidents. Here, unlike approaches to the prevention of adult accidents in the workplace (which, while still clearly sub-optimal, have made significant advances, as documented by O'Donnell (1990), Snashall (1990) and Stewart (1990)), the main thrust of child accident prevention continues to make heavy use of advice, safety campaigns and competitions for children to design posters, all punctuated with reminders to mothers that the main responsibility is theirs.

Little has changed in the past 90 years. In 1904, letters to the *New York Times* were suggesting that 'parents should realize that they are responsible for the child's life, and if they turn it out to play in a crowded street and it is run over they are . . . to blame' (quoted in Zelizer 1986). In 1992, a safety organization's catalogue showed a poster headlined 'Some parents don't care', issued educational materials reminding parents not to leave children alone and pointed out that accidents happen when children are over-protected, under-protected or over-tired – all factors squarely in the domain of sensitive parenting. 'Must do better' is the title of one recent report on child pedestrians in Scotland; 'Be seen and not hurt' is an injunction to child pedestrians in a recent advertising campaign.

The irony here is that the message of some of the educational and advertising campaigns of the Royal Society for the Prevention of Accidents (RoSPA) is out of step with that same organization's research and developmental work, much of which is conducted to a very high standard. This discrepancy is also apparent in other areas of health education. For instance the (then) Health Education Council (HEC) ran a series of advertisements in the early 1980s graphically 'educating' pregnant women on the dangers of cigarette smoking, showing babies in the see-through uterus of a smoking mother and so on. At the same time, work by Hilary Graham (funded by the HEC) told them that most mothers *know* that smoking is bad for them and for their babies (Graham 1984b). It is not the knowledge they lack but the means to act on it. The implication here is that it might be wise to look at the context in which dangerous behaviours occur in order to promote a more meaningful health education campaign. It may be that behaviours are constrained by material and environmental factors and cannot therefore be tackled in isolation. For example, while the emphasis of road safety work is especially focused on the child's behaviour, Ampofo-Boateng and Thomson's (1989) important review of current approaches to child pedestrian accidents in the UK suggests that verbal instruction to children (for instance, to 'look before crossing the road') can be hazardous when abstracted from the environment in which the child is operating. What are the limits to where a child can look, and what is a child supposed to do on the basis of what she or he sees?

Developing these lines of thought, there is, alongside the literature and advertising campaigns that present parents and children as frankly responsible for their own accidents, a research literature that offers a fundamental challenge to the premises behind the slogans. This research literature is what forms the starting point for our own study. We start from the premise that parents, especially those living in hazardous environments, probably know quite a lot about accident risks. Certainly, the research on which this book is based would never have been initiated had this not been the case. Policymakers working in the comfort of their air-conditioned offices might have a lot to learn from experiences at the 'coal face' and the accident education process might most realistically be seen as something that operates from the bottom up rather than from the top down.

Although there is evidence that parents and children rightly recognize their responsibility for their own bodies and their own lives, at the very local level there is also evidence that ordinary people are acutely aware of dangerous places and events in their day-to-day lives. This local knowledge is what current policy-making so often overlooks. Open any local newspaper and there will be parents asking 'Does there have to be a death before x or y is changed?', or sometimes, tragically, 'How many more deaths do there have to be before x or y is changed?' This kind of question makes us wary of a model of investigation in which the behaviour of the family and the child is scrutinized, found wanting and subjected to advice from 'the experts'. More interest could be afforded to the extraordinarily hazardous conditions in which many children, even in a fairly affluent society, live their lives. More research could target the poor performance of car drivers, the kitchens planned by people who have clearly never had to supervise a stove and young children at the same time, and architects who produce nifty looking balconies with enticing gaps at tiny tot level; these areas are not addressed with quite the same energy as is found in those producing materials to 'educate' children. Ironically, on the few occasions when the wider responsibilities for child accidents have been explored, the evidence produced has been inadequately used by decision-makers (Ranson 1987; Sinnott and Jackson 1990).

This book attempts to remedy the imbalance in our understanding of accidents by drawing on ordinary people's knowledge built up during the day-to-day routines associated with life in an uncertain environment. Linked to a health promotion or health education approach is a view that the experts will tell you what the risks are and how to manage them. But to what extent can the experts be expected to know what is happening, particularly in terms of local risks? And even in terms of global risks, it is worth remembering that the dangers of DDT were not brought to the world's attention by scientists, but by amateur ornithologists who had noticed that birds of prey were decreasing in number (Royal Commission on Environmental Protection 1989).

The death or injury of a child in an accident is a very personalized tragedy, as is the death or injury of a child through abuse. Currently, while the latter may not always be effectively addressed, it is at least addressed. Resources are directed towards this problem. It is an issue. Whole social work teams are active around child protection. In contrast, at the moment children's accidents are nobody's problem, except that of the parents, even though children's injuries are a problem, and a costly one, for the NHS, for the police force and for other public bodies.

When several children die in the same accident, there will be an outcry for a while: a call, perhaps, for safety belts on school buses or a tightening up of the rules governing school journeys. But most accidents to children are isolated events. One child is injured, or dies. Coroners' courts in England and Wales and the Procurator Fiscal in Scotland look at every child accident, but many of these child deaths are simply treated as 'accidental' and strategic planning to avoid similar events is not carried out. It is instructive that in this area popular television programmes such as *That's Life* will frequently have a faster, more immediate and more lasting effect on dangerous events or places than will those bodies whom one might expect to fill a vacuum in this area of child protection.

The lack of strategic attention and coordinated policy-making on children's accidents is discussed in more detail in the final chapter. But it is worth rehearsing here that, at a national level, accidents fall within the remit of a number of government departments, including the Department of Trade and Industry, where the consumer safety department produces annual home and leisure accident data, the department for Education and Employment, the Environment and Transport departments, the Home Office (with responsibility for the fire service) and the Department of Health. At a local or regional level, fire, police and ambulance services, health authorities and health boards, schools, the Health and Safety Executive and the trading standards departments of local authorities are all among those with some responsibility. The prime messages of many of these departments are directed not towards planners, architects, providers of public transport and car drivers, but towards children and parents. Social workers do not exercise surveillance over risky places and risky drivers in the same way that they exercise surveillance of risky families. The prime responsibility, they all say, rests with parents, usually mothers, and children. We suggest in the chapters that follow not only that this displacement is morally indefensible, but that it hampers the development of effective accident prevention policies.

Safety as a social value

This book on children at risk is devoted to an analysis of child accidents and to a series of suggestions on how these might best be monitored, managed and prevented. Our first aim is to draw attention to the extent of the problem: to make the point that when children are at risk they are most likely to be at risk from accidental injury or death. We therefore begin by exploring how the patterning of actual and potential accident risk might best and most usefully be established. Drawing on our case study research in Corkerhill, a housing scheme in Glasgow, we describe the social and spatial distribution of accidents and of unsafe events, places and behaviours. We aim throughout to uncover parents' own views about the nature and patterning of accident risks, and to elicit their ideas on why the steep social class gradient in children's accidents is as it is. Are working-class parents, as the literature frequently suggests, fatalistic about accidents, and if not, how do they conceptualize them and how do they deal with the challenges of living in unsafe environments?

Our study of child safety is mounted primarily from a sociological rather than an epidemiological or medical perspective. Our view of what accidents are is therefore a broad one, and our examination of the consequences of a locally high accident rate is similarly wide-ranging. In moving on to consider the effects of accidents, we are concerned, therefore, not just with injury but with perceived and actual vulnerability and with the worry and anxiety this may engender. Because of the preoccupation with the injury effects of accidents, we know little about their direct and indirect social and psychological effects. We know very little as yet about the long-term effects of accident experiences (though the Child Accident Prevention Trust initiated a study of this in 1994), and the health consequences of the anxiety generated by living with risk every day are also largely unexplored. Yet we might suspect these consequences to be far-reaching. Only half the children who sustain serious accidental head injuries, for instance, ever resume normal schooling (Heiskanen and Kaste 1974; Brink *et al.* 1980). Studies, like our own, that can explore the links between an accident, its real and perceived gravity and its wider consequences and effects may shed some light on this kind of problem.

After exploring the patterning of accidents and their individual and social consequences, we move on to consider some practical issues on the theme of accident prevention. We know that there has been a steep fall in child deaths from the other major childhood killers, such as measles, pneumonia, whooping cough and diphtheria. Our challenge now is to find ways to reduce the deaths and injuries to children from accidents, and to ensure that our children do not face accidents and injury as a result of entirely avoidable risks. In exploring these issues, we turn the normal questions asked about child accidents on their head. We are not as interested in asking 'Why did that child accident happen?' as we are in asking 'How is it, in the face of so many hazards to children, that most of them grow up safely?' Our interest in talking to parents, therefore, was not to ask 'What is it you do that puts children at risk?' but 'How do you manage to keep your children so safe for so much of the time?'

Our approach to collating materials suitable for accident prevention policy is thus 'bottom-up' rather than 'top-down'. We assume that parents encountering risks on a day-to-day basis, challenged every day to keep their children safe – and largely succeeding at the task – are well placed to know about risks, how they are managed now and how they might be managed more effectively in the future. We draw out from this information some lessons for planners and for those involved in the promotion of good health, both as parents and as professionals. In short, we aim to find more effective ways of using what people already know to prevent child accidents, to reduce the injuries associated with them and to bring the death toll down.

2

Child accidents in an urban community

Our aim in this book is to explore the antecedents, character, distribution and consequences of accidents and accident risks. Because accident event data are not the same as injury data, and are not routinely collated by any official body, we have based our empirical research on one relatively small case study area. Partly this reflects the origin of the project itself, which was initiated not by us but by concerned parents living in a high risk neighbourhood. However, this focus also allowed us to harness the case study methods of the anthropologist to the concerns of medical sociology and to use this, as well as surveys and statistics, as the basis of our generalizations.

The case study approach

In recent years there have been two opposing thrusts to the social research effort. On the one hand we have seen the advent of 'big' social science. This refers essentially to the building of large, linked data sets based on social surveys, official statistics and census data which cover large chunks of space and time and attempt to provide as complete as possible a picture of the social world. British examples include the British Crime Survey, the British Household Survey, the National Child Development Study and the panel survey 'Living in Britain'. This approach is one in which the model for social science continues to follow the model for natural science, attempting to find out as many facts as possible about the organization of social life. The idea behind this approach is similar to the idea behind, for instance, the human genome project. If we can only collect more and more information to a more and more detailed level we will have sufficient knowledge to understand our problems and find effective solutions, preventions or cures.

On the other hand, we have seen a renewed interest in the intensive case study approach to sociological analysis (Mitchell 1983; Hammersley 1992). This falls at the opposite pole to the extensive survey work described above. While both approaches aim to increase our knowledge of the social world, the case study method has some attractions over the large scale approach if our aim is to make progress in understanding, and ultimately preventing, child accidents. First, it is more geared to looking at the connections between interlinked events; second, it is more amenable to examining the meaning of events and circumstances; and third, even (perhaps especially) where case studies are selected for their *a*typicality they can yield insights that studies seeking to monitor the general, the average or the 'norm' overlook. Case study approaches are, moreover, suited to the application of a wide range of data collection techniques – both qualitative and quantitative – whereas 'big' social science tends to rely solely on the apparent objectivism of the social survey. Because we wish to take a broad view of accident events – regarding them as the intersection of a set of perceptions, actions and environments, rather than conceptualizing them in terms of their associated injuries – access to subjective as well as objective data is important.

Our project, therefore, uses a case study in an attempt to broaden existing quantitative and qualitative knowledge of child accident risks. The study area is a small council estate in Glasgow known as Corkerhill. Its key characteristics are outlined below.

Corkerhill and its people

Corkerhill was once described as a model railway village. It was established in 1896 by the Glasgow and South Western Railway Company with a population of 700, mainly railwaymen, all transferred from Dumfriesshire in southern Scotland. In 1900, the Corkerhill Railwaymen's Institute was established in the tradition of the Pullman model industrial villages near Chicago in the United States of America. The Railway Institute became the living heart of the community. It had a suite of baths, a library and recreation rooms. The town clerk gave his services free, as did the fire brigade and ambulance. There was a Rent Club, and members absent from work through sickness had their rent paid. There were frequent rail services to the city, to breathing spaces of the countryside and to coastal resorts like Largs and Saltcoats (Morrison *et al.* 1992).

Today, the population of Corkerhill has more than doubled, and its people live in a rather smaller area on Glasgow's south side. Corkerhill is bounded to the north by the Glasgow to Paisley railway line and rail yard, to the south by the River Cart, to the west by a fast main road and to the east by the neighbourhood's one amenity, an area of parkland backing on to Pollock Park, which houses the world famous Burrell Art Collection. The estate now accommodates 585 households, of which 209 contain children aged 14 and under. About 40 per cent of the households with children are headed by a single parent, although in some cases the other parent, usually the father, lives very nearby. Slightly fewer than half (46 per cent) of the households with children had only one child at the time of the interviews, a third had two children and the remainder contained three or more youngsters. The number of families with four or more children is higher than for the district and the region as a whole. Additionally, 38 per cent of parents said that there was a child in their household with a health problem that affected him or her on a daily or a regular basis. Overall, unemployment in households with children runs at some 14 per cent, and those parents who are in employment are largely in social classes IV and V. Only 42 per cent of such households have access to a car.

Households in Corkerhill tend to be rather young (with children) or made up of older people – 121 are in receipt of a state retirement or widow's pension. Most people who live in Corkerhill were brought up locally, and 15 per cent of householders have lived in Corkerhill all their lives. A further 90 per cent and more come from within ten miles of Corkerhill. At the time of our study in 1992 there was just one ethnic minority household in the neighbourhood.

The cottage houses which once comprised the village have now been demolished to make way for low-rise high density housing. Public transport has declined. The only communal facilities are the dismal one-storey community 'shop', a meeting room next door to the newsagent and, up the road, a 'tenants' hall'. From time to time these are transformed by hard work, nice tablecloths, good food and a warm welcome for parties, weddings, dances or funeral wakes. There is a chip shop ('the chippie') and a newsagent-cum-grocer. On the busy main road there is a pub – The Cart – named after the nearby river. The community has no doctor's surgery or school, but it recently got a neighbourhood housing office so that repairs can be negotiated, and rents paid, locally.

The glum recital of socio-economic hardships has become commonplace in descriptions of communities visited, studied or otherwise explored by social scientists. Yet, as will become clear below, Corkerhill, in common with many other disadvantaged and depressed communities, is not well served by labels referring to a lack of general well-being. These descriptions conceal a community with the normal share of joy as well as troubles and containing energized groups and individuals who are struggling to provide the best life possible for themselves and their children with an admirable degree of resilience.

Residents of the estate now live in four main housing types. There are flat roofed tenements, three storeys high with balconies, and pitched roof tenements, again three storeys high. The 'cream' of the housing stock in the area are the cottage style houses with gardens. Additionally, there are just a few 'four in a block' houses. By far the majority of families live in pitched roof tenements. The housing is not of a very high standard. Only 29 per cent of households with children reported that they had no problem with dampness in their housing, and 48 per cent of such households reported one or more rooms wholly or partly unusable as a result of damp.

Corkerhill has not, therefore, been transformed by the 'right to buy' policy, which has been in place since 1980 and which Forrest and Murie (1988) show has operated throughout Britain in a socially and environmentally selective way. The sale of council housing to sitting tenants has largely consisted of the sale of the better properties of the public sector, i.e. houses rather than flats, in suburban rather than city locations and in good condition, not in poor repair. The homes sold are those which make a good investment for their owners, not those where costs of maintenance and repair exceed the capital value of the dwelling. The buyers, too, have distinctive characteristics: they are the better-off tenants, in secure employment at the peak of their earnings careers. 'Right to buy' owners are not young or old households and they are not among those marginal to the labour market or dependent on benefits. Not surprisingly, given the characteristics of the population in Corkerhill, at the time of our survey only ten households were owned outright or being bought, and these are overwhelmingly the more attractive and safer cottage type houses.

Like all remaining public sector estates, however, Corkerhill is indirectly affected by the right to buy. Housing estates with more desirable housing than Corkerhill do have more houses transferring into private ownership, and those who have to rent must therefore move into those pockets of council and housing association housing which are unlikely ever to attract private buyers. Corkerhill is one such pocket, and like others of its type it is increasingly marginal to the mainstream of the housing system. Tenants are prone to being and feeling neglected, and to finding (though rarely accepting) that they have little power to affect their position.

Where the community is probably quite unusual relative to other Glasgow neighbourhoods is in the clear boundaries that separate Corkerhill from nearby districts. A surrounding of road, rail, river and parkland helps to define the neighbourhood and lend a sense of identity. Sadly, access to the parkland amenity is likely to become less possible in future, when the new M77 road route to Ayr is built, bringing some 40,000 vehicles a day within metres of the houses on the western periphery of Corkerhill, destroying woodlands and wildlife, and effectively cutting the community off from the green spaces of Pollock Country Park, Pollock House and the Burrell Museum.

Corkerhill as a case study

Although Corkerhill is a small housing estate in a large Scottish city in a society where every community, indeed every individual, is different, it contains information, experience and expertise that is of general interest. Unless we were to believe (which as social scientists, we do not) that there is no such thing as 'society', we can infer that there will be similarities between Corkerhill and its people, and other communities and their people. As Cathie Rice, one of our community consultants, has written,

> when community groups from similar types of area, be they in Glasgow, Manchester, Liverpool or elsewhere meet, there has been instant recognition of problems, and the types of responses given by individuals to those problems. Dampness could provoke responses such as 'these people make their homes damp so they can get a house near their mum,' or 'It's not dampness pet, it's condensation. Burn all your fires, keep all your windows open during the day, don't wash clothes, make soup or boil too many kettles. Oh and try not to breathe too hard in the bedroom.' Almost funny if you don't consider childhood asthma, ruined clothes, furniture and lives.
>
> (Rice *et al.* 1994: 145)

Moreover, the possibilities for generalization go beyond even communities with socio-economic and environmental similarities to Corkerhill. While the experience of parenting and being a child are very substantially mediated by class, ethnicity, gender and income (something we discuss in more detail elsewhere in relation to the social class gradient, gender and age difference in child accident deaths), there are also commonalties of experience. Keeping children safe in any environment is difficult. All parents, and all children, learn from experience, sometimes bitter experience. All of us, to a greater or lesser extent, know as parents or as people who were once children about the difficulties of keeping safe in environments which are more or less hostile to children. Corkerhill is an environment closer to the 'more hostile' end of the spectrum, but it is far from unique.

Corkerhill is certainly similar to other deprived urban areas. High unemployment, low car ownership, a deteriorating housing stock and poor local facilities are not only features common to many housing estates in Britain, they are also the sorts of indicators that have traditionally shown a close association with child accidents (Wadsworth *et al.* 1983; Pless *et al.* 1989). The social class gradient in child accidents is extremely steep and Corkerhill forms a good case study precisely because it contains many of the features associated with a high child accident rate. Additionally, because we are interested in how unsafe environments themselves generate safety knowledge that could provide a pool of information to be harnessed to safety campaigns, Corkerhill offers a good focus for our attention.

One aspect of this case study that is perhaps unusual is that the community approached the researchers rather than the reverse. This is by no means a unique circumstance (see Martin *et al.* 1987), but it is rather a different approach to 'selecting' a case study from what is commonly encountered in the literature. We did not initially choose to work in Corkerhill, then, because of its 'accidentogenic' character. We assumed, correctly as it turned out, that it would have a relatively high child accident rate. However, we worked there principally because we were invited to.

The origins of the project date from an approach by some of the area's tenants to Glasgow University. They were put through to Helen Roberts in (what was then) the Social Paediatric and Obstetric Research Unit, which was invited to collaborate in a study examining what parents viewed as an unacceptably high level of asthma among their children. The parents hypothesized not only that there is a link between the incidence of asthma and the condition of their cold damp homes, but also that there is a link between respiratory illnesses among adults, children and even pets and the chemicals used to 'treat' the mould.

The research unit was unable to assist with this particular piece of work, though we were able to put the community into contact with researchers in Scotland who had explored some of these issues (Martin *et al.* 1987; Hunt 1993a). As a result of this initial contact, however, other connections were made and in her capacity as an occasional freelance journalist on maternal and child health issues, Helen Roberts wrote a number of pieces about the community (e.g. Roberts 1989a, b). Additionally, a paediatric epidemiologist working in the same unit, David Stone, persuaded some local parents to take part in a video for health practitioners on the health effects of poor housing (Stone with Roberts 1992).

Before embarking on the accident project, then, people in Corkerhill had successfully (and sometimes unsuccessfully) campaigned on a number of issues over several years. The damp housing and the chemicals used to treat it were the subject of a 'Damphouse Enquiry', which resulted in a change of policy in the local authority. On another theme, parents astonished that immunoglobulin – needed to prevent hepatitis (and to alleviate the fear of hepatitis) following needlestick injuries – was not routinely and immediately available at the local accident and emergency department campaigned successfully to overturn existing policies (which required ordering for named patients, and therefore a day of waiting and worrying whenever a child accidentally pierced itself with a discarded needle). People from the community also strongly opposed plans for the new M77 motorway cutting their community off from Pollock Park, and attended a public enquiry daily for six weeks to make their views known. While the road was not, as the community had hoped, diverted (a nearby golf course would apparently have been affected), they were told that as 'compensation' a new play area would be built.

Other achievements, especially in the field of community safety, have been secured in Corkerhill through the workings of the local community council. In Scotland, one of the tiers of local government is the community council established as a result of the Local Government of Scotland Act of 1973. These are non-political bodies whose purpose is to make community views known on local issues. This is of course done with a degree of activity and energy that varies over time and between communities. Corkerhill is undoubtedly at the very active end of the spectrum, with a number of extremely energetic individuals, including four who were to play a major part in the genesis and implementation of the child accident project.

The four individuals who most helped to launch and implement the project on which this book is based are Janice Coia, Walter Morrison, Betty Campbell and Cathie Rice. Janice Coia is a young mother who has campaigned relentlessly for the community over a number of years, and who was pivotal in the Damphouse Enquiry. In the early phase of our work, she was a ready source of information and other resources vital to setting up a project of this kind. Walter Morrison, the secretary of the community council, is the father of adult children, and has fought hard for his community in dozens of battles, as a result of which he does not have a large fan club among Glasgow politicians. Betty Campbell is a local mother and grandmother. Her husband was killed in an unprovoked attack not long before we started our work in Corkerhill. She has recently become chair of the community council, and she runs a safety group for children in the area. Betty Campbell and Walter Morrison were helpful to the project in a variety of important ways, ranging from 'advertising' the research, organizing meetings and helping us to maximize our response rate to keeping the 'community shop' warm enough during a Glasgow winter to prevent our interviewers succumbing to hypothermia, providing endless cups of tea and organizing child care during our group interviews. Cathie Rice was chair of the community council at the time the work was carried out. She had two children at the start of our involvement in Corkerhill – three by the end – and supported and contributed to the research in many ways, including facilitating our work with young people and speaking at meetings.

Over a number of years, community safety and child safety had been part of the agenda of the community council in Corkerhill. Early achievements of the community council in the 1970s and 1980s included the establishment of a pedestrian crossing on the busy Corkerhill road, fencing by the river and pedestrian barriers for the protection of young children on their way to the local primary school. Although community safety was not, in all honesty, at the very top of the agenda in a community with a variety of pressing problems from poor housing to low incomes, and from ill health and disability to unemployment, safety issues were important and they were conceived of in a context far wider than we might have originally imagined. A strength of the research, from our point of view was that it ran alongside a concerted action campaign by the parents. We also hope (and believe) that from the community's point of view, the research assisted the campaigns and might continue to do so.

Although such direct and deliberate interplay between the research project and local interests could be seen as bringing bias or distortion to the data, local commitment to the work in the end proved essential to its success, and for us it marked a major strength of the undertaking. As Hunt (1993b) has pointed out, people who live in communities like the one we worked with have grown rather tired in recent years of the teams of researchers who come in to look at this or that. In addition to the welfare professionals driving in and out of the estates, those carrying out research can frequently feel like one more imposition, one more call on the time of people for whom time is a real resource and, in the frequent absence of paid work, a means of exchange. One of our community consultants, Cathie Rice, draws attention to the same phenomenon as Sonja Hunt.

> In common with community organisations elsewhere, we in Corkerhill do of course recognise that the professional research body may be able to take information through doors which the community cannot open, but we have learned to be cautious, if not downright suspicious, of those who would 'assist' us in this way. Too often, we have been subjected to the 'goldfish bowl' approach to research. We have been researched upon. The researcher selects the topic, studies his subject, and returns to the lofty towers of academia leaving a bemused community who very soon realise that they have gained nothing from the experience. Despite this apparent cynicism, not only do we recognise the need for good research and the powerful potential it may have, but we are confident enough to believe that we have a contribution to make to it.
>
> (Rice *et al.* 1994)

The Corkerhill parents' campaign around child accidents is, then, essentially community led, and local people are partners in this research in more than a superficial sense. Often, the role of social scientists is seen by professionals and politicians as one that assists them – the experts – to understand why people behave in ways they do not expect. Why do people continue to smoke, drink, cross dangerous roads and eat high fat foods when all the evidence suggests this is bad for them? The same idea is currently embedded in a lot of ideas about accident prevention. The question everyone wants us to ask is why people take risks with the health and welfare of their children.

In this study, the role of the social scientists was different from the outset. It was to assist the community to place its own views on the agenda. It was to help ordinary people establish why their needs are not recognized or met by those responsible for urban safety and child protection. It was to try to use local knowledge and expertise to work towards an effective suite of accident prevention policies. From a practical perspective, therefore, the local community was intimately involved in the planning and organization of the work; theoretically, too, the research is founded in the experiences of the community; and materially the group respondents have, wherever possible, been properly compensated. While our research was a low cost project, we see no reason why community involvement should be a way of getting expertise on the cheap.

Having said this, it would be unrealistic to suggest that the interests of the academics and the community coincide at every point. There are different interests at stake, and while at one level members of the community may have an intellectual curiosity, as we do, in safety as a social value, their more pressing concerns are naturally focused on immediate rather than longer-term strategies for reducing accidents. Nevertheless, there is an important contrast between our work and the community action studies of the 1960s and early 1970s, in that whereas the earlier work (initiated, for instance, as part of the Community Development Projects) tended to result in a flow of initiative from the researchers into community action, our project is just the converse, with the community taking the initiative to stimulate the involvement of the academic community.

The community recognizes the need to make alliances with decision-makers, policy-makers and implementers, as well as academics, if the project is to be more than parochial in the very strict meaning of the word. The community group is, for instance, actively trying to forge links with the district and regional councils, from whom it hopes to obtain some modest funds and, equally importantly, to make the high level politician and officer links that will enable the successful elements of this project to be used and adapted elsewhere in the city.

The community (and indeed the researchers), however, has had to recognize that the behaviour of local decision-makers, politicians and professionals is subject to social constraints, just as those living in Corkerhill are subject to constraints. The concept of the public *servant* is no longer fashionable, and decision-makers may develop a top dressing of matiness and consultation while holding their own closed meetings away from the community and making the important decisions there. We hope, as researchers, that we have put ourselves in a position not just to understand the problems of local people but also to analyse and understand some of the constraints and dilemmas facing politicians, policy implementers and those involved in promoting the public health. Accordingly a number of expert and professional groups whose work and responsibilities bring them into contact with Corkerhill have also been drawn into the project, including the local police, the health promotion department of the health board, workers with young people and drugs and the local health council.

While the community and the researchers always knew that the product of this research would not appear in the form of a knitting pattern for safety, we do aim to use it to design a framework for safety at home, at play and in transit at the community level. This combination of the research project and the parents' action group is one we feel may be an effective way of producing local safety data, exploring practical ways of putting our findings into practice and disseminating them to other communities in the city.

So, as a case study Corkerhill offers some things that are important because of the community's uniqueness, and some things that are important because it typifies low income neighbourhoods in a socially divided society. We hope that in the course of this book we will provide sufficient detail to enable the reader to judge for herself or himself the extent to which Corkerhill's experience is generalizable. Our view is that Corkerhill's similarity to many other communities means that the majority of our conclusions and recommendations are valid well beyond this one small community. Moreover, the common features of being a parent or a child almost anywhere in Britain lead us to feel that much of what we found has a relevance for child safety in general, and not just child safety in disadvantaged housing estates with high unemployment, poor housing and widespread lone motherhood.

On the other hand, while we do argue in our final chapter for some common recommendations based on our work, we do not wish to argue that Corkerhill is just the same as every other community. Our thesis is that many of the prerequisites for bringing children up safely are very highly locality based. Parents, and indeed children, are extremely well placed to use their own expertise and their local knowledge to develop accident prevention strategies. We describe in this book both the process and the results of an investigation of the ways in which children are kept safe (and why parents sometimes fail) in one particular community. Most importantly, perhaps, we describe an approach to eliciting locally relevant accident information that is relatively simple, relatively cheap and easily replicable in other locations.

Putting ideas into practice

In the opening chapter of the book we identified four key features of our approach to the study of child accidents. The first is to build up a census of all accident events, whether or not they result in injury or harm. After all, prevention should be based on a study of the causes of all hazardous events, not on information about the consequences of an arbitrarily defined subset of these. Second, we want to look at near accidents as well as accident events themselves, on the assumption that we can learn something about how children are kept safe by looking at how accidents are averted. Third, we aim to explore all these events qualitatively as well as quantitatively, because people do not live their lives with reference to the neat parcels of information that are packaged into survey responses and official statistics. Finally, our data are intended to facilitate ways of monitoring and managing accident risk that build on local knowledge. With these aims in mind, we conducted the work in three phases.

First, we conducted *a series of group interviews with parents and teenagers* with child care responsibilities. These interviews were designed to provide information on the nature, causes and consequences of accidents that would be useful at every stage of the project. They were intended to help us develop an inventory of the kind of things people regard as accident risks, and they provided an insight into the association between certain risks and the occurrence of an accident or near accident. They were also designed to provide some ideas about how accidents are conceptualized, experienced and dealt with in the lives of local people. They were conducted to help the researchers grasp something about the meaning of accidents in an unsafe environment, and to glean some sense of how accidents are positioned in people's minds alongside the other risks and uncertainties they have to cope with on a day-to-day basis.

Hedges (1985) points out that group interviews have much to offer to research in which 'the social context is important', when understanding and insight (rather than description and prediction) are required, when the work has an 'action research' component and when the interviews are part of a process of generating new ideas. These conditions all obtained at the outset of the research and with our need to explore 'the realities of everyday lives as they are experienced and explained by the people who live them' (Burgess *et al.* 1988: 310).

Group interviews are also well attuned to the spirit of our research, which not only recognizes the authenticity and value of local knowledge, but also seeks to 'democratize' the research process. Group interviews have a strength in this respect since they allow the people involved to negotiate among themselves and to make their own collective generalizations about the topic at hand. This contrasts with the more conventional model in which analysts interview a range of people separately and then retreat to their offices to draw out the commonalties and resolve the differences themselves.

The group interviews, additionally, help to advance our interest in the concept of safety as a *social* value; that is, as a quality of life which is defined, sought after, developed and maintained, by whole communities or societies. Individual views and practices are important, then, not simply for what they achieve for that individual and their immediate family, but also for the way they shape, interact with and are themselves mediated by the views of others. Group interviews are an important vehicle by which this process of interaction and negotiation can be monitored.

There are, of course, some disadvantages with the group-based approach, and these are itemized by Hedges (1985). The most challenging of these concern the tendency to subsume individuals into the life of the group, absorbing minority or hesitant voices to the will of the majority or dominant voices, and encouraging individuals to play a role, or put on an act. These are important problems. But they are not insurmountable in the context of the research reported in this book, where group interviews have a very specific role in a much wider project: they are not a substitute for random samples where generalizations about a population are required; and they are not a substitute for individual interviews where the primary aim of the research is to catch a glimpse into personal details and private thoughts.

Although in designing the group interviews we did not seek representativeness in a statistical sense, we did take steps to ensure that as wide a range of views as possible was included in this part of the research. Thus, five types of group were targeted for interview.

One group of (predominantly) mothers was drawn from each of the three main housing types in Corkerhill: those living in pitched roof dwellings, those in flat roof housing and those in cottage type dwellings. The distinction between housing types was chosen because the relationship between dwelling design and accident risks was one of the main concerns of the Corkerhill residents who initiated the research. Moreover, while Corkerhill is itself a post-war estate, it was built in several phases. The pitched roof and flat roof developments are older, and they are all flatted accommodation. The flat roof dwellings are generally in the worst condition, while the more recently built cottage dwellings (houses with gardens) are of better quality and more sought after.

In addition to the parents' groups, we interviewed a mixed group of teenagers. Teenagers, it was felt, would be young enough to remember accidents and near accidents that they themselves had been involved in, but would be old enough to have begun to take on child care responsibilities themselves (for instance, by acting as babysitters for parents and other relatives). Finally, to get a perspective from other people with a responsibility for child care, but without the responsibility for routinely maintaining safety on a day-to-day basis, a group of professionals was convened, comprising two health promotion officers, a fire prevention officer, a health visitor, a housing manager, a community police officer and a road safety officer from the council's roads department.

The aim at the outset was to interview each group of six to eight people three times for between 45 and 90 minutes (except the professionals, whose interview took the form of one meeting). This means that most of our interviews were more concerned with what Burgess *et al.* (1988) call 'in-depth small groups' than with 'once-only groups'. Our aim here was not to 'enable participants to understand themselves better, and to develop or change some part of their professional or personal behaviour' (Burgess *et al.* 1988: 312). It was, rather, to allow a certain degree of familiarity to grow up between the interviewers and interviewees; to allow a common understanding and appreciation of a range of local problems to be developed. This strategy was important: all the groups 'worked' better in the later interviews. It was to prove vital in our meetings with the teenagers, who did not really begin to speak freely until the last session.

In contrast, in the group convened with the professional workers the gap between interviewers and interviewees was much narrower, and while the practicalities of convening the same group of professionals more than once meant that a second interview was never planned, in fact a single interview was sufficient to cover all the necessary ground. This group was also of a kind where 'the interpersonal relationships of the members are secondary to the discussion of the product' (Burgess *et al.* 1988: 311).

The characteristics of the group interviews are summarized in Table 2.1. The interviews with parents and teenagers were usually conducted with two of the three authors and took place in Corkerhill (though the professionals met at Glasgow University). The interviewees were recruited for us by Corkerhill residents (the professional group was organized by the researchers). This meant that (in contrast to the process of recruiting the professional representatives) we had no direct control over precisely who came to the interviews. We did, nevertheless, specify broadly what kind of person was needed for each set of interviews (ideally the parents were to have children now or to have brought children up in the recent past while living in Corkerhill).

Table 2.1 Group interviews in the Corkerhill study

	Number in group	Average number of years in Corkerhill	Number of meetings
Parents, flat roof homes	9	12.6	3
Parents, pitched roof homes	4	21.7	2
Parents, cottage type homes	8	15	3
Teenagers	6	9.5	3
Professionals	7	none live there	1

The group interviews with parents and children each lasted around two hours, and each week – as confidence grew – we were able to tackle more and more sensitive issues concerning accident risks. In the opening interview, questions centred on ideas about what accidents are and who is at risk from them. We asked questions like 'what do you think of when you read about accidents, or hear people talking about them?' We then asked what kinds of accidents are most common in Corkerhill and which ones concern people most. In the second interview, we asked more specifically about where local accidents tend to happen and about what promotes safety and what puts children at risk. We talked about why some areas and features were safe or unsafe, and we discussed ways of reducing danger. In the final interview, we asked about the worry that accidents can provoke. Parents told us about the ways in which they respond to the threat of accidents and how they cope with anxiety concerning the children's safety. Finally, we considered the things people would do to try to make things safer if they had unlimited funds, if they had a relatively small sum of money and if they had no extra resources at all.

In the professionals' group interview, we tried to cover the same kind of ground as with the parents. We also asked specifically about some of the issues the parents had raised with us. However, a rather different approach was taken with the teenagers, who had little to say about the kinds of events we had thought of as accidents. Nor did they respond well to the notion of safety or safe-keeping. In the end, we asked them what our opening question should be. 'Ask us about our scars', they replied. So we did, and it resulted in animated and detailed information about a number of accident events. We recommend this question for future work.

The group interviews provided us not only with information directly relevant to our understanding of child accidents, but also with the knowledge we required to construct an interview schedule sensitive to local needs. Group interviews do not in themselves provide the kinds of materials we need to build up a census of accident events, but the information they yielded meant that when it came to employing larger scale quantitative approaches, we at least knew what to count. The group interviews were not designed to make statements about the incidence and experience of accidents and related events throughout Corkerhill, but the prevalence study which formed the second part of the research was. Because this survey was designed with the group interviews in mind, we were able to ask not only questions that appealed to us as social scientists, but also those that only people living in Corkerhill could have formulated.

The group interviews thus fed directly into *a household survey implemented to establish the prevalence of child accidents and near accidents in the community as a whole.* Because Corkerhill is a relatively small community and accidents are relatively rare events, we attempted to interview all households on the estate. Although we used a shorter interview schedule for those without children, we knew that many older people had brought children up on the estate and had useful perspectives on safety and danger in the area. In the end, we succeeded in speaking to 95 per cent of all households with children of 14 and under and 84 per cent of households without them, and so secured an astonishingly high response rate (see Figure 2.1). This high level of cooperation is partly a function of local interest in the topic, and partly a consequence of the intensive effort both the researchers and the community put into the interview process. Notably, a researcher was on hand (based in the community shop) to answer questions throughout the interview period and members of the community council collaborated closely with the interviewers to facilitate access to interviewees. It is also possible (and we hope likely) that the high completion rate and detailed answers associated with the questionnaires were achieved at least partly because the questions were often based on local ideas and seemed relevant to local concerns.

Initially, we planned to use local people to conduct the household survey. A number of parents were experienced interviewers, having already carried out a survey into health problems related to the anti-mould chemicals used to treat damp housing. Their involvement at the interviewing stage would have been in line with the move towards 'popular epidemiology' now occurring in the USA (Brown 1989, 1990), but the strategy is far less common in Britain. The use of local interviewers may have helped the response rate (though in the end it was high even without this) but it might also have limited the use of some of the more sensitive questions on the schedule. In the end, discussions with our community consultants and with other individuals and groups within the neighbourhood led us to adopt the more conventional approach. While people in Corkerhill maintain a healthy scepticism about what professionals can achieve, there was a strong feeling that the work would have more impact, and be taken more seriously elsewhere, if professional interviewers were employed. We therefore took on eight interviewers with experience in health research, some with nursing backgrounds, and provided supplementary training targeted to the needs of the project.

The main aim of the survey was to provide population-based data on accident prevalence in a specific community, by asking about actual experiences of accidents over a given reference period. As a recall device these were divided into accidents requiring hospital admission, accidents requiring hospital attention, accidents resulting in a visit to the GP, accidents where attention was not sought from a medical source but there was some injury and to attend to accidents where there was no injury and near accidents. In addition to this accident census, the survey was designed to provide representative data on factors that frustrate the accident chain, by

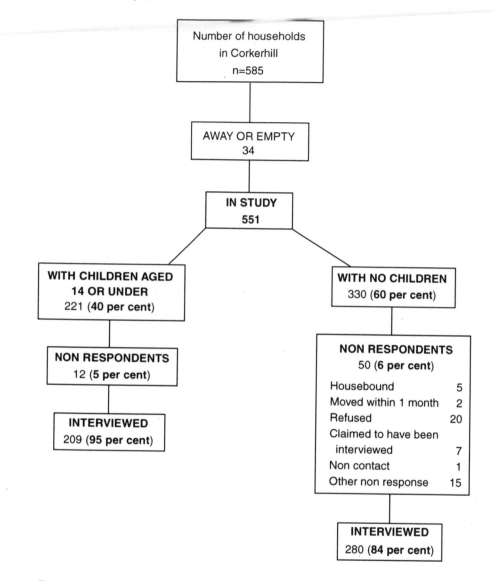

Figure 2.1 Accident census: survey response rates.

asking about the circumstances surrounding near accidents occurring over the same reference period. Finally, the survey was used to elicit information on aspects of the home and neighbourhood that are hazardous and thus likely to lead to accidents.

The household survey contains valuable information on the incidence of accidents and near misses, on the extent of danger in the local environments,

Table 2.2   A profile of case study interviews

Case number	Gender	Incident	Age of child	Location of accident	Precipitating factor
1	boy	near miss	toddler	inside	socket
2	boy	accident	primary B	outside	football
3	girl	accident	pre-school	outside	barbed wire
4	girl	accident	secondary	outside	roller boots
5	boy	near miss	primary A	outside	traffic
6	girl	accident	pre-school	outside	dog
7	boy	near miss	primary A	outside	traffic
8	boy	accident	primary B	inside	couch
9	boy	near miss	primary A	outside	traffic
10	girl	near miss	baby	inside	baby-walker
11	girl	near miss	pre-school	inside	socket
12	girl	accident	primary B	outside	traffic
13	boy	near miss	primary B	outside	fall
14	boy	accident	primary A	inside	tapwater
15	boy	near miss	primary A	inside	fire
16	boy	accident	toddler	inside	tapwater
17	girl	accident	toddler	outside	pavement
18	girl	near miss	toddler	inside	window
19	boy	near miss	pre-school	inside	window
20	boy	accident	pre-school	outside	garden
21	boy	accident	primary B	outside	scaffolding
22	girl	accident	pre-school	inside	iron
23	girl	near miss	pre-school	outside	traffic
24	girl	accident	toddler	inside	bunk bed
25	girl	near miss	baby	inside	veranda

Note: primary A refers to 5–7-year-olds, primary B to 8–11-year-olds.

on people's reactions to accidents and on the steps they take to minimize risk. It also provides the raw material for the third phase of the research, namely *in-depth studies of a set of accidents and near accidents that children have experienced, and parents have dealt with, in the past year*. We explored circumstances preceding, surrounding and following 25 accidents and near misses among children from 15 families. The characteristics of these incidents and of the children who experienced them are given in Table 2.2.

We examined 13 accidents and 12 near misses from ten two-parent and five single-parent households with children whose ages ranged from a few months to 14 years. The families were chosen to give a representative mix of ages, sexes and the type of accidents and near misses reported during the survey. In formulating the interview checklist we consulted with health promotion, clinical and other colleagues with an interest in prevention in order to ensure that the data we collected would have some salience for those working in policy and practice.

The narratives secured during this part of the study help to contextualize the quantitative data on the antecedents and effects of accidents that were collated as part of the household survey. These interviews provide a vivid glimpse of how parents incorporate safety issues into their daily routines, and of the problems that arise when these routines are interrupted or compromised by hazardous places and events. They show when, where and how parents anticipate accident events (and also why they sometimes do not); they illuminate the scope parents have (and do not have) to intervene in accident events; and they illustrate some of the far-reaching consequences that living with and experiencing risk have on parents and children alike.

Conclusion

This chapter has introduced the case study that forms the core of our discussion of accidents and accident prevention. We have argued that a case study approach is a useful one given the current state of knowledge and understanding about the epidemiology and sociology of child accidents. Much of what we write in the following pages is therefore based on the experiences of the residents of Glasgow District Council's Corkerhill estate. These experiences are in one sense unique, and in another sense entirely representative of the experiences parents, children and the wider society encounter anywhere in Britain, and indeed in any developed society. All young children are at risk, and all parents spend much of their time trying to keep their family safe. If we have anything new to learn about this, it is, we might argue, most likely to be rooted in the lives of people whose risks are greatest and whose means of managing danger are ostensibly most limited. This, at least, is the premiss we adopt. In the chapters that follow, we use this rich store of experience to illustrate where and why accidents occur, to examine their immediate and long-term effects and to consider ways of preventing them. While the data we draw on are specific to a particular place at a particular time, it is our contention that the ideas they generate and the practical recommendations that flow from them are much more widely applicable.

3

Monitoring risk

A census of child accidents

A key rationale for studying child accidents is to build up a picture of who is at risk, when, where and why. Official statistics are not adequate for this task, especially where information is required on accident events rather than on particular types of injury or areas of health service demand. A key component of the collaborative project that forms the basis of this book was therefore the collection of information on accidents of all types and severities, including events that were averted or did not result in an injury. The aim was to compile a unique census of children's accidents in a single locality over a one-year period, and to use this to provide new insights into the cause and distribution of accident events. This census was contained within the household survey described in Chapter 2, and here we use those materials to analyse a variety of accident events and build up a picture of the risks built into children's everyday lives.

This chapter begins by exploring the extent to which accident events are patterned, with a view to using this information as the basis for formulating (in Chapter 5) an effective approach to accident prevention. We go on, in the second part of the chapter, to consider parents' wider views about the origin, nature and distribution of accident risks.

While questionnaire surveys have a number of attractions for those wishing to sell newspapers, or chart the fortunes of baked beans, attempts to use the same methods to make political predictions before general elections tend to cast doubt on the universal reliability of this approach. Questions asked in social surveys, or in 'big' social science, can obscure as much as they reveal. As Graham (1983, 1984a) has pointed out, the social order of the survey is one of 'units' and 'cases'. These units in everyday life function as individuals, households and streets. Surveys work to the extent that individuals can formulate the required information as answers to questions formulated by the investigators. Aspects of social life that cannot be shaped into answer-sized pieces are lost.

Although we did need to use a social survey approach, in order to obtain one type of accident data, the design and content of this survey depended heavily on the insights and observations we had gleaned through our group interviews, which formed the opening phase of the work. We use findings of these qualitative interviews more directly in much of the rest of the book. Below, however, we discuss the main findings of the household survey which is based on them, in order to provide a quantitative account of the geography, sociology and epidemiology of child accidents on the Corkerhill estate.

The census of accidents included serious accidents (those resulting in a visit to the doctor, a trip to an accident and emergency service or a hospital admission), less serious accidents (those resulting in an injury which was treated at home), non-injury accidents and near misses. These occur with different frequencies (serious accidents are much less common than near misses) and generally fit into people's memories unevenly (an accident that results in a few days in hospital is more memorable than a graze treated at home). Therefore we asked about them in different ways and over different recall periods.

For *serious accidents* parents were asked to recall all events that had occurred during the past year. The one-year period was defined in the survey as between New Year 1991 and New Year 1992. New Year (1 January) is a clearly defined moment which people in Scotland can easily relate back to and as the survey was conducted between January and March it was a relevant benchmark to choose. We expected parents to have fairly accurate recall of these types of accidents over a one-year period, not only because they are a relatively rare occurrence for a single household even in a high risk area, but also because they had required medical attention away from home, which often involves a great deal of organization. It is also possible that this kind of accident would be regarded as the most severe by parents, who often suffered considerable anxiety and, as we were to discover, implemented lifestyle and environmental changes as a result.

There was a total of 162 'serious' accidents recorded for the one-year reference period. The overall accident rate for serious accidents was therefore 0.43 per child per year in Corkerhill. In fact, however, the 162 serious accidents were sustained by 113 children, which gives a rate of 1.4 events per 'accident-prone' child. Table 3.1 shows the distribution of accidents among the children involved.

Overall, in the one-year period in Corkerhill one-third of children were victims of what could be described as a serious accident. Three-quarters of

Table 3.1   Distribution of 'serious' accidents among children at risk over one year

Number of accidents per child	Number of children	Percentage of all 'accident-prone' children experiencing an accident at the given frequency
1	85	75
2	17	15
3	7	6
4	3	3
10	1	1

Note: For reasons that we have discussed, it is difficult to derive the 'seriousness' of an accident simply from event data. We therefore defined as a 'serious' accident one for which medical or dental treatment was sought.

these had a single serious accident, with a further 15 per cent having two accidents. Seven per cent of children had more than one serious accident and 3 per cent had multiple serious accidents. Of the 11 children who had multiple accidents one child had ten, involving eight trips to his GP and two to an accident and emergency department.

The most common accident for which medical attention was sought involved cuts and lacerations, followed by bruises and crush injuries, abrasions, swellings, lumps and bumps and fractures. Less common but more serious problems included burns and scalds, poisoning and concussion. While medical colleagues reading this list might well question the 'serious' label, these were sufficiently serious incidents to have brought the child to the attention of a medical or dental practitioner. The incidents were thus considered by parents to be of an order that justified the investment of time needed to seek attention, and such work as there is on this suggests that parent reports are very reliable (Agass *et al*. 1990).

It is difficult to compare these statistics with published accident data as figures for the number of children taken to their family doctor following an accident are not widely available. Comparing the Corkerhill data to discharge data (bearing in mind the drawbacks outlined above) for Glasgow nevertheless provides a useful indicator. In Corkerhill during the year 1991–2 there were a total of 14 children admitted to hospital following an accident. In Glasgow as a whole an average of two children per 100 are admitted to hospital as the result of an accident. For an area the size of Corkerhill it would therefore be expected that seven children per year would be admitted following an accident. The figure of 14 that we elicited is thus twice the Glasgow average. This figure is high but not altogether surprising given the steep social gradient in children's accidents (Avery and Jackson 1993) and the fact that Corkerhill falls toward the lower end of the economic ladder.

In addition to being asked for information on severe accidents, parents were asked about the number of *accidents treated at home* in the previous week (the week before the interview). Again this question was asked for each child in turn. The one-week recall period was chosen because it was expected that the number of accidents treated at home would be higher than the number referred to the health services, and it was assumed that the accuracy of recall of these minor, almost routine, events would diminish more steeply over time. Our aim in adopting the very short period of one week was to persuade parents to recall even very minor accidents. We wanted to know about incidents whose management is regarded as a routine part of everyday parenting.

Of the 373 children in the survey a total of 112 (30 per cent) had been involved in at least one accident that required treatment at home during the week prior to the interview. Between them these children experienced 315 accident events. Of the children concerned, 55 per cent had a single accident with 11 per cent and 12 per cent having two and three accidents respectively. The remaining 32 children (28 per cent) had four or more accidents. The figures are given in Table 3.2.

Children are often involved in events that have all the harmful characteristics of an accident but do not result in injury. They are also exposed to a variety of potentially hazardous situations – series of events that appear to be leading to an accident but are interrupted before harm or injury occurs. These *non-injury accidents and near misses* are rarely documented in accident research, but they could contain important clues on how accidents arise and on the most effective ways to avert them.

Anticipating that parents would have more difficulty in answering questions about non-injury accidents and about near misses than about injury-producing accidents, we asked only for examples of when such events occurred. We asked for these to be selected from the experiences of all the respondents' children, at any time in their life. Almost a third of parents

Table 3.2 Accidents treated at home

Number of accidents per child	Number of children	Percentage of all children having an accident treated at home
1	55	49
2	12	11
3	13	12
4	6	5
5	5	4
6	6	5
7	8	7
8	7	6

(30 per cent) were able to recall at least one non-injury accident and 47 per cent recalled at least one incident where an accident was averted at the last minute. Fully 60 per cent believe that their children often have other near misses that they never get to hear about, indicating that parents are more than aware that their children end up in potentially risky situations but that most of the time an accident does not result.

The accident census shows that although accident events are rare in children's lives when compared with all the times they are safe, they are much more common than people tend to assume. One in three children has a serious accident in any one year, nearly one in three has a minor scrape every week and half the parents know of at least one memorable near miss in their children's lives. Accident events are common, then, if we compare them to their more newsworthy counterparts of child abduction and abuse. On the basis of this evidence, we would not argue that the latter merit less attention, but that the former merit more.

A social geography of accident events

So far, we have documented the extent of accident events and near misses in the Corkerhill district. The accident rate is above average and accident-related events are widespread. The fact that the rate is above average can be accounted for with reference to a range of larger scale studies. There is a body of psychological and sociological work, for instance, which has identified links between accidents and particular family formations, unemployment, stress, maternal depression and a variety of other factors (Sibert 1975; Brown and Davidson 1978; Wadsworth *et al.* 1983). Research has also documented the extent to which environmental factors and dwelling conditions affect vulnerability to a range of risks (Littlewood and Tinker 1981; Ranson 1987; Lowry 1990; Sinnott and Jackson 1990). In general, the evidence is that low incomes, poor housing, single parenthood, above average family size and overcrowding are all indicators of accident risk.

Corkerhill scores above average for Glasgow on the main risk indicators, and it is hardly surprising that overall it has an above-average accident rate. Knowing the environment the parents are coping with, we might well expect it to be higher. In a housing system where neighbourhood quality varies according to ability to pay, low income families are likely to end up in hazardous living conditions, including a generally accident-prone environment. However, by examining variations in accident risk within this vulnerable environment, safe-keeping strategies that are effective for this and other localities might be identified.

Our next aim is therefore to consider whether and how accidents are distributed or patterned both spatially and socially. First, we sought to establish whether or not there was any statistical evidence for a systematic rather than random distribution of accidents among the households on the estate. We looked at this question by comparing the distribution of accidents per child in Corkerhill to a theoretical distribution. The appropriate theoretical distribution is not one which assumes that accidents are spread equally – this is not what happens when things arise by chance. What is required is a distribution that is suggestive of a random generating process – the kind of process that might account for the incidence of accidents if they really were a question of good or bad luck. The appropriate distribution for this exercise is the Poisson distribution. This distribution gives approximations to the frequency of occurrence of relatively rare, randomly generated, discrete events.

Accidents, as we have measured them so far, *are* discrete events: if they occur independently of one another and independently of any underlying systematic causal factors, we might expect them to be distributed among children approximately as indicated by the Poisson distribution. Accordingly, Table 3.3 compares the actual distribution of both serious accidents and accidents treated at home with the patterns to be expected if they had arisen randomly. The overwhelming message from the table is that the distribution of accidents treated at home departs significantly from this expectation. More children than expected remained safe, and more than expected experienced multiple accidents. We would have expected 43 per cent of children not to have an accident, when in fact 70 per cent managed successfully to avoid such risk (which suggests that there is some very successful safe-keeping happening in the neighbourhood). We would have expected 5 per cent of children to have three or more accidents, but in fact 12 per cent proved especially accident-prone. There are some aspects of risk, it seems, that some parents and children find consistently difficult to avoid. The differences between the observed and expected patterning of accidents could have arisen from recall and reporting biases, but if not they suggest that some home environments or lifestyles are systematically more likely than others to provide the setting in which an accident might arise.

The distribution of serious accidents matches the Poisson distribution a little more closely than does the distribution of accidents treated at home. This might suggest that some kinds of accident – possibly those with the most serious consequence – are fairly random in occurrence. However, we should also consider the possibility that the element of randomness arises from decisions about whether or not to contact the statutory services, rather than from factors determining whether or not an accident event happens.

In the light of this indication of at least some non-random elements in the incidence of accident events, we looked at some of the factors that might be associated with a heightened exposure to risk, both overall and among

Table 3.3   Are accidents distributed at random?

Number of accidents per child	Accidents at home		Poisson distribution (expected percentage)	Serious accidents		Poisson distribution (expected percentage)
	Observed			Observed		
	Number	Percentage		Number	Percentage	
0	258	70	43	260	70	65
1	55	15	36	85	23	28
2	12	3	15	17	4	6
3	13	3	4	7	4	1
4+	32	9	1	4	1	1

Note: Numbers and percentages are of children.

certain individuals and households. Because Corkerhill is a small community without wide variations in income or environmental features, we did not, of course, expect to be able to document the level of social and spatial variations in accident risk that a national or even city-wide study might show. However, given the possibility that some children are significantly safer than others, even within a generally high risk neighbourhood, some attempts to explore the data further seem warranted.

To this end, we initially distinguished families where there had been at least one serious accident from those where there had been none (during the previous year) and cross-tabulated the resulting dichotomous variable with a number of socio-economic and environmental indicators. Low income and overcrowding were significantly associated with accident risk, but none of the other indicators, including single parenthood, unemployment and any of the environmental factors, proved important. We extended the analysis by looking at the correlates of the accident rate per child (per family). This allowed us to control for household size. Income and overcrowding remained significantly associated with serious accident risk, and unemployment proved important too. Even within a relatively homogeneous area, then, economic inequalities are aligned with inequalities in accident risk.

A number of attitudinal and behavioural variables were also examined. Given the limited explanatory power of the socio-economic variables, and in the light of the emphasis on behavioural change and health education that pervades current accident prevention policy, it might be thought that they would be significant. On the whole, however, attitudinal and behavioural differences failed to discriminate between parents whose children had and had not recently experienced an accident event. The only notable attitudinal difference is that parents of children who had experienced a serious accident were significantly more likely than others to state that they considered Corkerhill to be unsafe or very unsafe for children. This, of course, is a consequence rather than a cause of the differential accident risk.

The accident census contained questions not only on who experienced an accident and when, but also on where the accident occurred and why. Parents were asked to give a very detailed account of one accident event in each of the categories of serious accident, accident treated at home, non-injury accident and near miss (where appropriate). In each case, parents were ask to select the most serious event. The additional information included where the incident happened, what the child was doing at the time, what went wrong (in the parent's opinion), what caused the injury, what the child's injuries were and any precautions or changes of routine that had been implemented as a result of the incident.

While the social distribution of accidents is important in giving insight into the nature of risk inequalities, the spatial distribution may offer further clues to the explanation for these inequalities. In general we found that the kinds of places where accidents happened were around the house: in the back court, in the close, on the veranda; in the kitchen, living room or bedroom; on the scaffolding, window ledge or roof; or in the school playground. The kinds of things the child was doing at the time were the kinds of things children do: playing with a brother, sister or friend, playing on their own, helping their mum in the kitchen, 'mucking around', climbing, swinging or 'being curious'. There seemed nothing out of the ordinary in the behaviours of accident-prone children. The problem seems to have arisen where 'normal' behaviours encountered an unsafe environmental setting.

This geography varied little according to the severity of the accident concerned, though those involving the statutory services were slightly more likely to have occurred in a public place. Of the 12 incidents requiring hospital admission during the study period, six happened in the home, five in the street or play area and one outside the immediate area of Corkerhill. Of those events leading to hospital admissions more than a year before the interview, i.e. outside the main study period, 45 per cent (13) happened in the home and almost a third (31 per cent, 9) in the street or play area. Over a third (35 per cent, 23) of accidents that resulted in a trip to accident and emergency happened in the street or play area; just under a quarter (24 per cent, 16) happened in the home; and 29 per cent (19) happened around the home (on the stairs, in the close, in the garden areas). The remaining 12 per cent (8) happened further afield, including in schools, on buses, at relatives' or friends' homes outside the area and at the swimming baths or golf course. The figures are collected in Table 3.4.

For the largest group of accidents – those involving a visit to the GP – the majority occurred in the street, with a further quarter occurring at home. Almost half of the accidents treated at home happened in the home, with a

Table 3.4 Environments of risk

Type of accident	Location of accident							
	Home		Wider home area		Street or play area		Further afield	
	Number	Percentage	Number	Percentage	Number	Percentage	Number	Percentage
Admission	6	50	0	0	5	42	1	8
Admission over one year ago	13	45	4	14	9	31	3	10
Visit to A & E	16	24	19	29	23	35	8	12
Visit to GP	11	27	8	20	16	40	5	12
Treat at home	40	44	12	13	24	26	15	16
Total	86	36	43	18	77	32	32	13

Note: Percentages refer to row totals. Row data refer to accidents requiring hospital admission in the study year, similar accidents prior to the study year and accidents requiring treatment at accident and emergency (A & E) departments, by a general practitioner and at home (all in the study period).

further quarter happening in the street or play area. Among the factors implicated in these are falls (including from one level to another and on the stairs) and being struck by an object, person, animal or bike. Hamsters, dogs and cats were also cited as hazards leading to accidents treated at home.

Looking at where the accident happened by age group, not surprisingly we found that younger children have more accidents in the home and that the older children get the greater the proportion of their accidents which occur out of the home. The relationship between age group and location of accident is shown in Table 3.5.

Table 3.5 shows the locations of all the accidents we monitored: those resulting in admissions to hospital, trips to accident and emergency departments, trips to the GP or dentist and accidents treated at home. For children under one year of age all the reported accidents happened at home or around the home, whereas over half the accidents reported for children aged between eight and ten years of age happened in the street or play area. The greatest number and proportion of accidents happening outside of the area happened to those aged 11–14 years. For this age group over a quarter of their accidents occurred outside Corkerhill.

Knowing something about the aetiology of accident events is, of course, just the first step in being able to identify the underlying risks and precipitating

Table 3.5 Age of children involved in accident events

Age of child	Location of accident							
	Home		Wider home area		Street or play area		Further afield	
	Number	Percentage	Number	Percentage	Number	Percentage	Number	Percentage
Under 1	6	55	5	45	0	0	0	0
1 to 4	78	42	47	25	55	29	3	2
5 to 7	18	15	31	26	56	47	12	10
8 to 10	7	11	15	24	34	55	6	10
11 to 14	8	15	3	6	26	50	14	27

factors. The next section of this chapter goes on to consider some qualitative and quantitative findings that cast further light on the causes of the accidents described above.

Conceptualizing accident risk

Some communities are more vulnerable to child accidents than others, and within those communities some households are more at risk than their neighbours. How can we begin to understand these differences? As a starting point, we have to acknowledge that life is a risky business and that simply to live, play and enjoy their world, children from all backgrounds and in every environment will encounter some hazards. Second, it is worth emphasizing that children are especially vulnerable in an adult-oriented world. For the most part we do not gear the environment to the needs of children, and safe-keeping activities are no different from any other in this respect. Some countries (e.g. Sweden) have a better record than others (e.g. Britain), and governments do have some scope to alter this element of the 'background' risk that all children in their society face. Our main concern, however, is not with either of these sets of general risk factors. It is rather the unequal distribution of risks which occur over and above these background levels that we seek to address.

It is our view that recognizing inequalities in accident-proneness is an important aspect of the conceptualization of accident risk. This is, first, because risk inequalities are not necessary or inevitable – they are part of a political choice about where and why resources are targeted. Second, it is because reducing inequalities in the distribution of accident risks is likely to be the most effective strategy for reducing the overall accident rate. For instance, Roberts's (1993) work shows that child pedestrian death rates have fallen as car ownership has increased because more children travel by car and are therefore kept off the streets where they might be at risk from motorists. But there is a socio-economic gradient in car ownership which sets crucial limits to the protective effect of the increased use of motor vehicles. The child pedestrian death rate in the lower social classes has not declined on a par with that of children from more affluent families, because they are simply exposed to an increased volume of traffic. High death rates from the children most at risk are thus now the limiting factor on bringing the overall accident death rate down. The same principle holds true across a number of types of accident risk. As Popay and Young (1993: 24) point out, seemingly obvious strategies to reduce risks across the board might not work quite as anticipated.

> Parents with less money may buy poorer quality safety equipment or none at all. The risk to their children will therefore remain either the same [as that of children in higher socio-economic groups], or be reduced to a lesser extent. The same argument would apply to fireproof furniture, for example, or to the provision of safety advice not accessible to people whose first language is not English.

Adams (1985, 1988a, b) also makes the point that achieving a fairer distribution of risks is the key to meeting overall accident prevention targets.

Factors associated with the unequal distribution of risk operate first with respect to whole communities, and second with respect to differences between the households in those communities. What is it about low incomes, council renting and other indices of deprivation that links them with a high risk of accidents? What is it about life in one part of the estate rather than another, in one kind of council tenancy rather than another, in one set of family forms rather than another, that makes children in some households particularly at risk?

In one sense, of course, it is a question of how you look at it. Reasons for differences in accident rates are seen very differently depending on where you are standing. For a single parent living three floors up, having no backdoor and garden in which her children can play safely may be the most important factor in the likelihood of one of her children having an accident while playing on the stairs or in the street at the front of the house. For a professional the overriding factor may be the fact that the children are allowed to be out on the stairs or in the street unsupervised. These two perspectives illustrate how one set of circumstances can be viewed very differently by people in different positions, with very different consequences for the kinds of prevention strategy they might lead to.

During our research we attached great importance to how parents conceptualized accident risk; not because we feel that theirs should be the only voice, but because it is a voice that has too often been ignored or silenced. The parents in Corkerhill were asked whether or not certain factors contribute

Table 3.6 Adults' views of the factors that predispose children to accidents (percentages)

| Predisposing factor | Is the listed factor important in accounting for child accidents? | | | |
| | Households with children | | Households without children | |
	Yes	No	Yes	No
Housing quality	75	25	53	47
Local environment	89	11	73	27
Poverty	73	27	63	37
Children's behaviour	68	32	70	30
Parents' attitudes	63	37	73	27

to the greater number of accidents in Corkerhill compared to Bearsden or Newton Mearns (both middle-class housing areas). The responses, shown in Table 3.6, suggest that parents widely view the local environment as a major contributor to the high number of accidents. Three-quarters of parents think that the housing in Corkerhill contributes to the high accident rate and almost three-quarters feel that poverty is also an important underlying factor. Parents are a little more likely to express this view than non-parents.

Table 3.6 also illuminates a paradox that runs through this study, which is that although the group interviews, the individual interviews and the survey itself emphasize the importance of environmental risk, local people generally, and mothers in particular, tend, when comparing themselves with their more affluent counterparts, to fall back on explanations relating to people and their inadequacies. Thus parental attitude is identified as a significant source of the different accident rates between the two communities. This is partly a reflection of parental guilt (which we discuss later) and partly a reflection of the idea that a minority of local parents – quite definitely 'not like us' – do put their children at risk.

Parents were also asked if there were any other factors that might account for the higher number of accidents in Corkerhill. Fifteen per cent of parents said yes, with the roads, traffic and lack of facilities being the most often cited. Although there are differences in priority between those who have children in the household and those who do not, both groups agree that the factors identified here contribute to the differing accident rates between their community and a more affluent area of the city.

Professionals' opinions, as we observe in several parts of this book, generally tend to differ from those of parents. Yet, although the discussions we held with them were heavily focused on behaviour and the need to change it through education, there was also some recognition of the need for safety equipment in a dangerous environment, and of how parents in areas like

Corkerhill would have problems finding the money to buy even the basics. This discussion shows that the professionals acknowledge that parents find it hard to keep children safe because of the design of the neighbourhood. As one of the group, talking about the balconies on many of the flats, put it: 'I mean I really can't understand why there aren't more kids going over the top of these things.'

The indication, then, is that, from the point of view of those most responsible for keeping children safe, hazardous living environments rather than any attitudinal, behavioural or educational deficiency on the part of the parents is what accounts for discrepancies in the type of risks that underpin inequalities in the accident rate. This is borne out by other recent research, which now emphasizes the importance of the environment over behaviour in understanding the geography and sociology of accident risk. When Bijur *et al.* (1988a) explored the effects of overcrowding on accident rates they found that environmental differences between families of varying size accounted for the association between accident risk and family size. When Blume (1982) considered the links between social class, morbidity and mortality, they all proved to be highly correlated with bad housing, unemployment and low income. Other environmental risk factors are identified in the work of Dougherty *et al.* (1990), whose study of motor vehicle traffic accidents revealed a rate of injury in the poorest neighbourhoods as much as four times that in better off areas. Sunderland (1984) also concluded that it may be the environment rather than the child that is accident-prone after studying the social gradient of children's traffic deaths in Sheffield. The same kinds of observations can be gleaned from local people's answers to questions about the possible causes of accidents in Corkerhill.

Parents were asked to recall the precipitants of individual accidents as well as to discuss their wider underlying causes. Generally the kinds of things that went wrong ranged from pure chance (wind blew foreign body into eye) to daring or dangerous behaviour on the part of the child (set fire to bin; jumped from van; dared to walk along window ledge). There was also dangerous behaviour on the part of others: motor vehicle didn't stop; speeding car mounted pavement; bite from a pet dog or hamster; found needles and syringe or was jagged by needle. Sometimes there was reference to what we normally think of as an accident: fall on one level; fall from one level to another; fall through glass door. Sometimes there was a failure of supervision: swallowed medicine/whisky/anti-freeze; jumped into hot bath. Sometimes there was an institutional or organizational failure: glass fell out; open manhole.

Although the antecedents of child accidents consist of a range of behaviours interacting with a range of environments, it is clear that, for virtually all accident types, the commonest failing is associated with some aspect of the outside fabric of the area: the stairs, pavement, fences, outside

Table 3.7   The causes of known accident events

Cause	Type of accident				
	Hospital admission in study year	Hospital admission, ever	Accident and emergency treatment	Visit to general practitioner	Treatment at home
Hot liquid	1	5	1	0	0
Outside fabric of area	4	14	43	25	58
Toys etc.	0	1	4	2	10
Household equipment	1	6	12	7	17
Noxious substances	4	1	1	0	0
Vehicle	2	2	2	0	0
People	0	0	2	2	3

Note: Table entries refer to numbers of accidents.

walls, hedges, bins and any other similar feature. The range of immediate causes of accidents is shown in Table 3.7, which also indicates where the various injuries caused were dealt with.

All accidents involving hot liquid required treatment at hospital, as did all accidents involving a motor vehicle or noxious substances. On the other hand, the greatest number of accidents treated at home were caused by some aspect of the fabric of the area. Most of these injuries were cuts and bruises that are considered part of growing up. Aspects of the built environment of the area were also responsible for 66 per cent of the accidents that ended up in accident and emergency departments. After the fabric of the area, household equipment is responsible for the next greatest number of accidents – both those treated at home and those ending up at accident and emergency departments. This group includes furniture, glass, scissors, knives, cookers, heaters and any other similar household equipment.

The distribution of the causes of accidents by the age group of the children involved is also of interest. This is shown in Table 3.8. All the accidents involving hot liquid happened to children aged seven or under, with the majority happening to children aged between one and four years. This is not surprising as it is generally younger children who knock over cups or pull over containers of hot liquid. For these younger children accidents involving hot liquid are more serious because of the ratio of their body size to the liquid. Accidents involving noxious substances are also concentrated in the

Table 3.8   Accident causes by age of child involved

Age of child (years)	Cause of accident						
	Hot liquid	Outside fabric	Toys/ sports equip- ment	House- hold equip- ment	Noxious sub- stance	Motor vehicle	Another Person
<1	1	3	0	0	0	0	0
1–4	5	54	7	23	4	4	1
5–7	1	44	5	10	2	2	2
8–10	0	23	3	6	0	2	1
11–14	0	21	2	8	0	2	4

Note: Table entries refer to numbers of accidents.

younger age groups. Again this would be expected as older children are more aware of labels and know about dangerous substances. Conversely, accidents involving another person are more often seen in older age groups. This would be linked through play and recreation activities.

As a consequence of experiencing these types of accidents, parents are acutely aware of the features of their homes that threaten their children's safety. A total of 67 per cent (140) of parents say there are dangerous things within their homes. Their views are shown in Table 3.9. Of most concern is some aspect of the windows: 45 per cent of the parents who identify dangers inside the home recognize that there are problems here. The windows are considered dangerous because they are ill-fitting, have no safety catches, open easily or have rotten frames or sills. Problems with the electric sockets are mentioned by a further 13 per cent (18) of parents, including the lack of on/off switches and their positioning. Other features, mentioned by fewer parents, include the temperature of the water (which they are unable to regulate), the kitchen design or position within the house, glass in internal doors, dampness inside the home, open fires without guards and hot pipes. In short, parents do not need more information about this kind of risk – they can clearly identify the character and location of most of the hazards within their homes.

When asked about the outside of the building, including communal shared areas, parents overwhelmingly consider these to be characterized by their dangerous features. A total of 166 (79 per cent) parents gave examples of potentially dangerous features around the buildings. The greatest concern is the verandas, which are seen as hazardous by 63 (38 per cent) parents. A further 49 (29 per cent) mentioned the more general problem of the upkeep of the area, including the amount of rubbish and debris lying around the buildings and in the back courts; they also mentioned ill-tended back

Table 3.9 Parents' views of the risks built into their homes

Feature	Parents who say each feature makes it hard to keep their children safe		
	Number	Percentage of all respondents (n = 207)	Percentage of those who say their home is unsafe (n = 140)
Windows without locks	67	30	48
Generally unsafe windows	23	10	16
Electric sockets	29	13	21
Verandas	25	11	18
Damp	18	8	13
Unguarded fires	15	7	11
Unsafe doors	12	5	9
Other design faults	18	8	13
Kitchen layout	10	4	7
Other	9	4	6

gardens and a generally poor state of repair. Problems with broken glass were frequently mentioned, and at least part of this is the responsibility of housing repair teams who replace broken windows but who – according to our interviewees – frequently knock the remains of a broken pane into the back court or garden and do not clear it up when the job is finished.

Finally, parents were asked to think about the wider environment of Corkerhill and to identify any features of it that could be considered a danger to children. This question raised a resounding answer of yes, with 92 per cent (192) of parents giving examples. Over half of the parents (53 per cent) think the greatest danger is some aspect of the roads, including the volume of traffic, speeding vehicles and lack of traffic calming within the scheme. Other aspects that concern local people are the railway line which borders Corkerhill, the inadequate provision of play areas and the local drug problem (which leads to used needles being dumped in the closes).

Parents are, therefore, all too aware of the dangers their children potentially face in their home, around the home – where it should be safe to play – and in the wider area of Corkerhill. And in formulating this awareness, they provide a conceptualization of accident risks that roots risks firmly in the environment and its interaction with lifestyle constraints. The different kinds and sources of risk identified by parents can be grouped loosely into four categories.

1 Elements of the physical environment: easily accessible flat roofs that children tend to play on; open verandas with space enough for toddlers to

crawl under or youngsters to climb over; stone steps which easily ice over in winter; dangerous window fittings and badly designed kitchens, and so on. These were by far the most prominent causal factors identified within the community.

2 Risks introduced by poor management and organization in the locality: careless workmen, unsympathetic officials and inflexible bureaucracies.

3 Risks associated with the problems parents have in balancing child care with other responsibilities and demands on their time.

4 Risks that remain a threat because people simply cannot afford to deal with them. Family finances are often stretched in Corkerhill, and even in the area of expenditure on child welfare there are many competing demands (food, heating, clothing), which may compromise purchases required for safe-keeping.

Parents do not, it seems, need educating about the type and distribution of these hazards, and their behaviours are already geared to them. So the evidence of the census of accidents in Corkerhill points to the importance of environmental management over health education as the key to bringing down the child accident rate, and as the key to reducing inequalities in the distribution of accident risks. This is confirmed in our more detailed investigation of how people living in Corkerhill conceptualize risk.

It would be easy for local people to see risk largely as a matter of fate or chance – something inevitable which, like the damp, the mould and the roaming dogs, folk just have to put up with. It would also be easy to respond to accidents simply by taking care of injuries rather than by thinking about their wider antecedents and consequences. As we see in the remainder of this chapter and in Chapter 4, this is not what happens in an area like Corkerhill.

The group interviews with parents and children that were the starting point for our work may well be more likely to illustrate shared views and values than the more individually oriented surveys or case studies. In practice, however, the views we collected by different mechanisms (and with different personnel: Helen Roberts, Susan Smith and Michelle Lloyd for the group interviews, trained interviewers for the survey and health visitor interviewers for the case studies) gave remarkably similar snapshots of people's views of accidents. They raise at least three important points.

First, the 'accidental' nature of accidents is robustly challenged by local people. Accidents are predictable in the light of the way the environment has been shaped. The houses, for instance, 'are no designed with safety in mind at all, and yet they tell you they're family houses.' With metal sinks with sharp corners, no safe cupboards for cleaning materials, permanently live power points and flat roofs accessible to youngsters, accidents are seen as an inevitable, yet entirely predictable, eventuality. As one discussant points out,

Most of the architects that build these houses are men – young men in their twenties and that – and the day they're qualified, they go into design, but they don't realize – they don't have a clue about having a family and different things.

'These houses,' someone continued,

should have been built in Saudi Arabia, no here. Definitely no here. They're no styled for here. We don't get the weather here for them. They are just single brick as well, so it's no just the window that's taking the heat away. You've only got the one brick. So it's only lagging and the roof you can do. You cannae do that with a flat roof.

It became clear from the group interviews with lay people in Corkerhill that the prevailing view is that with a little more planning, a little more thought, a different order of priorities, the area could be a much safer place. Accidents are therefore seen as not 'accidental' at all.

Second, and perhaps even more striking, *local people see accidents as part of a seamless web of uncertainty*, on a par with, and inseparable from, illness and other risks of living in cold damp housing. Asthma, for instance, is seen as one of the main health risks afflicting the community, and our lay groups would constantly answer our questions about accidents with comments about asthma. While the conventional wisdom of social science methodology and group interviewing might suggest that we should have kept a tighter grip on the subject matter, ensuring that it did not stray from our primary concern, accidents, by exploring what they had to say we learnt a great deal about the way in which people who live in the community experience risk.

It is, for instance, quite plausible that for the high proportion of children whose health is giving their parents cause for concern there is an impact on their vulnerability to the risk of accidents. Asthma and other respiratory problems were reported in well over 40 children. Other health problems reported range from hearing difficulties to cystic fibrosis, from leukaemia to epilepsy, 'fits' and convulsions. Heart problems, kidney disease, bedwetting, learning difficulties and cerebral ataxia are all represented, along with various syndromes, infections, chronic ailments and difficulties such as speech defects. Moreover, 31 children (14.8 per cent) were reported by a parent to be unable to do things that most children of the same age can do because of a health, development or behaviour problem. Twelve children (5.7 per cent) were reported to need more help than usual for children of their age with feeding, dressing, toileting, walking, going up and down stairs or other daily activities. Fourteen (6.7 per cent) attended special school, or a special or remedial unit of an ordinary school, because of health or behaviour problems, disabilities or learning difficulties. Twenty-two

(10.5 per cent) attended an ordinary school, but were limited in taking part in school activities because of health or behaviour problems or disabilities. The parents of 49 (23.4 per cent) reported that children's health, behaviour or development caused worry that they might have a long-term health problem, physical or mental disability or handicap.

Child health problems are represented in neighbourhoods of every type, but such a high concentration of child health problems within a very small geographical area emphasizes the problems with which parents bringing up a child in Corkerhill have to contend. One strong recommendation from the lay groups for increasing safety was to have pitched roofs on the houses, and to improve the general state of housing. When one of us remarked, 'I can see how it would improve the general quality of people's lives and so on if you could put pitched roofs on the houses, but I'm not sure how it would make for a safer community, make it safer for children,' we were briskly reminded:

> Well you are doing away with the asthma for a start. There's an awful lot of kids in here with asthma because of the damp houses . . . And when your house is rotten with damp, and you're having to paper and paper, and you don't have the money to do it . . . When you're like that in that state, you're no attentive to your kids all the time . . . You're inclined to neglect the weans a bit because you've got that much pressure on them through lack of funds, but again, if the council [did its job], you wouldn't need all those funds to pay for paint every three or four months.

Likewise, depression was generally seen as a significant risk factor:

> You're back to that carry on where you've got depressed mothers who cannae be bothered making the effort . . . because they are depressed. They cannae be bothered washing their face and combing their hair to go out. We all go through it. I know I've been through that stage. By the way, I take it we've all been through it. It's hell.

The women were especially conscious of the stress placed on single mothers in this kind of environment.

> I really feel for single parents. It's hard enough when there's two of you, and you can at least sympathize with each other or have a good argument and feel better. If you're there on your own, the frustration must be absolutely terrible, and I think that's where people will turn round and talk about bad mothers. 'It's the mother's fault . . .' But it's no just as simple as that. It's a whole complicated thing and it's no just 'you're a bad mother.'

Third, accidents were most definitely not viewed fatalistically. It is frequently supposed that a strong barrier to effective accident prevention is fatalism. Health educators seem particularly prone to feel that those most at risk of accidents (those in social class V) are particularly prone to fatalism, and take it for granted that if an accident is going to happen, it's going to happen. We, however, found no evidence of this at all. We asked parents whether they agreed with the statement 'There's nothing you can do to stop accidents. They just happen.' Fully 61 per cent disagreed that this is the case, including 25 per cent who strongly disagreed. Those who *did* appear to hold fatalistic attitudes often did so more as a psychological coping strategy – a way to handle the ever-present risks – than as a substitute for preventive action. This is clear from the fact that parents are broadly supportive of the idea that more time should be spent teaching safety in schools. More than 90 per cent of parents favoured the idea of more time being spent on safety education for children, and although we express elsewhere our own reservations about this strategy, parents' enthusiasm for it certainly does not support the hypothesis that they take a fatalistic view of accident risks.

To summarize, our review of the character, frequency and distribution of accident risks in a high risk zone focuses our attention on the following issues. First, although the dominant view in policy circles conceptualizes accidents as a consequence of poor education and unsafe behaviours, the extent of the knowledge base and safety motivations in Corkerhill suggest that, in order to tackle accident inequalities, it might be more helpful to conceptualize accidents as a product of the interaction of environmental risk with local safe-keeping strategies. Second, while the reduction of death rates nationally is an appealing health target, the most effective accident prevention strategies are likely to hinge on tackling the uneven distribution of accident-proneness, and not just the overall child accident rate.

In this chapter, we have tried to identify the aspects of risk that might be said to mark preventable inequalities. In doing so, we have drawn attention to problems stemming from poor environmental management and low household incomes. In the next chapter we go on to show that actual accidents – whether 'real' or near misses – are only one consequence of living in a high risk area. The effect of accidents is more than injury, and the consequences of living in a high risk community spread far beyond the victims and their families. The real cost of accidents cannot be appreciated or tackled without prior consideration of these wider effects.

4

The social costs
of accidents

Accidents are a hazard to children's health and welfare, and a drain on health service budgets. This, however, is not the full extent of their impact on social well-being. This chapter considers the broader effects of child accidents, and of the risk of such accidents, on the quality of life and peace of mind of parents and the wider community. This wider social cost of accidents is not easily quantified, but since our aim, following Manciaux and Romer (1991), is to broaden the prevailing view about the effects of accidents, quantification may not be the most appropriate strategy. Our findings – which in fact draw on both quantitative and qualitative data – challenge the current preoccupation with the health and, especially, injury consequences of accidents and focus attention squarely on the wider social costs of risk. In this chapter we use the experience of households in a high risk community to show just how far reaching these wider costs can be.

In the literature to date, even the broadest view of the costs of accidents couches them in terms of financial outlays. This marks a welcome move away from the direct costs to service agencies of accident events (CAPT 1992) to include, for instance, the knock-on effects for household budgets of having a child in hospital for a particular period of time. Although this is a helpful alternative to focusing almost exclusively on the costs to the health services of accidental injury, we found that accidents have many more consequences for the quality of life of the communities in which they occur and for the welfare and well-being of the individuals involved.

In exploring these consequences, our study shows once again that it is important to differentiate between general and locality-specific explanations, and we argue that the effects of anxiety, like the prevention of the accidents that provoke it, might best be tackled by building on local knowledge rather than by invoking national norms. In order to develop this argument the chapter considers, in turn, the nature, distribution and origins of anxiety (including a discussion of the reasons why parents fear for their children), and the individual, community and societal consequences of living in fear.

The geography and sociology of anxiety

Most of the existing literature on worry and anxiety in urban settings refers to fear of crime. Some of the key arguments associated with this literature are reviewed by Smith (1987, 1989). Authors have pointed out that there is a difference (in the origins of the emotions and in their social consequences) between awareness of risk, on the one hand, and fear and anxiety on the other. Whereas people who are concerned about problems and aware of the risks can use this information to take preventive action, people affected by fear and anxiety may find it more difficult to tackle problems, and to cope with uncertainty. Awareness of risk is an important prerequisite of effective prevention; fear and anxiety can be debilitating conditions that affect people's judgement and impair their safety routines.

Because of this difference between the enabling function of realistic risk awareness and the disabling consequences of irrational anxiety, research on the fear of crime has become important in its own right, and public policy has been concerned with managing fear as well as with developing strategies for crime prevention. The aim has been to find ways of minimizing fear while maximizing risk awareness. Our study suggests that a similar two-pronged approach may be relevant to the promotion of child safety, though our view is that unless accident risk awareness (which is anyway well developed) is effectively coupled with opportunities for taking preventive and avoidance strategies, the net result is likely to be heightened fears and a continuing high accident rate. This is because when people are aware that risks exist but have no means of removing or avoiding them, the only solutions are crippling anxiety or a degree of resignation that some might mistake for complacency.

Like fear of crime, anxiety about accidents is much more widespread than the distribution of recent victims might suggest. Although just under half (96/209, 46 per cent) of Corkerhill's families experienced one or more serious childhood accidents in the study year, the majority of parents worry most of the time that their children might be involved in some kind of accident. This is apparent from Table 4.1, which shows the proportion of parents who worry about the possibility that their children will be involved in an accident while at home, in the street or at school. Four in every five parents worry about the safety of their children in the street, and over half worry about them in the ostensibly safe environments of the school and the home.

Table 4.1 Extent of worry among parents when their children are in different parts of the local environment

Location of child	Worry all or most of the time		Worry sometimes		Rarely worry	
	No.	Row percentage	No.	Row percentage	No.	Row percentage
At home	73	35	36	17	100	48
In the street	128	63	33	16	42	21
At school	36	21	52	31	81	48

Note: Row totals vary because different numbers of children are associated with each of the different locations. For instance, six children are too young to be allowed into the street, and 40 do not yet attend school or nursery.

For many parents, worrying about the risks their children face is a constant drain on their psychological resources. 'Ma heart's burnt out,' one mother told us. 'You're going, "Oh my God that wean's gonna get hit by a motor if he moves." That's how I'm grey haired.' In total, over three-quarters (76 per cent) of parents think Corkerhill is very unsafe for children. As they put it, 'You've just got to watch them [the children] constantly . . . you're constantly on the alert . . . you need eyes in the back of your head.'

Within Corkerhill worry about accident risks is widespread. It does not vary noticeably according to socio-economic status, gender, age or experience of parents. What, then, lies behind it? We found that fear and anxiety arise partly from the direct experience of accident events, and partly from parents' awareness of the sheer number of accident risks built into their local environment. Both sets of causal factors are considered below.

Both the qualitative and the quantitative data collated during our research indicate that the high levels of anxiety expressed by Corkerhill's parents are at least partly accounted for by their direct experience of accidents. In this sense, anxiety about accidents can be seen as a rational response to real risks. Families with children who have experienced one or more serious accidents in the past year are much more likely than other families to feel that the local environment is unsafe for children (84 per cent of the former but 68 per cent of the latter hold this view).

Near accidents have similar emotional consequences. Nearly half those interviewed are aware of near misses involving their children and these are twice as likely as other parents to worry all the time that their children will have an accident at home. Likewise, nearly three-quarters of people whose children have had serious near misses, compared to just half of the remainder, worry all or some of the time when their children are in the street. In a high accident risk area, then, we can expect high levels of parental anxiety, rooted in a real threat to the well-being of their children.

The qualitative interview data show in some detail how people learn from their own accident experiences to be fearful in unsafe environments, and it is clear from what our interviewees told us how the memory of a serious accident might engender fears for the future. Talking about their emotions around the time of an accident, parents made comments like:

I was absolutely petrified . . . I was absolutely paralysed.

I was really terrified . . . I was so frightened because he could have been dead or burned really bad if I hadn't caught him . . . I panicked and was afraid.

I totally panicked . . . all the time he was screaming and I was shouting shut up and thinking My God, what do I do?

[I was] terrified that the two of them were going to be lost in one minute . . . My husband was the same . . . you get such a fright.

Many parents said their main response to their child's accident was anxiety rather than panic. We asked a parent describing an accident, 'Did you panic?' She replied, 'Not really . . . Just fright and worry.' Another mum said her main thought was 'I better watch him from now on because this can happen so easily . . . and [I began to find myself] actually worrying about him.'

In short, it appears that in a high risk area you always know, as a parent, that an accident could happen. When it does, one possible result is that it makes you more fearful for the future. This is certainly one of the dominant consequences of child accidents in a place like Corkerhill. Here, high rates of anxiety about accidents are directly related to first-hand encounters with accident risks. Such anxiety is not, in that sense, unfounded or irrational. It is, however, partly a consequence of having such limited scope to prevent the same thing happening again, and in that sense, as we shall see, it is both a consequence and a cause of the inadequacies in accident prevention policy.

Anxiety about accident risks is not, moreover, only the result of having experienced an accident event directly. Such anxiety is clearly enhanced by concern about those aspects of children's living spaces that parents know build unnecessary hazards into their day-to-day lives. Thus, although the vast majority of parents interviewed believe Corkerhill to be very unsafe for children, parents alarmed, for instance, about permanently live electric sockets, poorly designed kitchens and derelict back courts are even more likely than others to believe that their neighbourhood is hostile to children's well-being and safety (Table 4.2).

Overall, nearly half the parents (103/209) believe their living space is so dangerous that their children are at risk of having a serious accident in the home, nearly two-fifths of parents think the design of their home is a major

Table 4.2 Environmental risks and perceptions of safety

Environmental feature	Is it a problem? (Who is afraid?)			
	Yes	(Percentage afraid)	No	(Percentage afraid)
Electric sockets	118	(79)	73	(71)
Window locks	116	(83)	85	(64)
Kitchen design	72	(86)	136	(70)
Back courts	135	(81)	55	(66)

Note: Percentage figures refer to the proportion of each group who believe Corkerhill to be very unsafe for children. For example, 79 per cent of the 118 people who identify electric sockets as risk factors, but just 71 per cent of the 73 people who don't, believe their neighbourhood to be very unsafe.

impediment to keeping children safe, and four in every five parents see the areas adjacent to their dwelling as dangerous. 'See the likes o' our type of house. See, the kitchen's very small an' narrow . . . you're afraid it could cause an accident.'

Those sensitized to risk in this way experience a disproportionately high incidence of anxiety about domestic accidents. 'A'm terrified aw they verandas an' they stairs,' observed one group interviewee. 'Ma worst fear,' noted her friend during the same discussion. The same is true for worry about accidents in the street. Over three-quarters (76 per cent) of those ($n = 107$) who see local dangers as a major problem interfering with daily routines, compared with fewer than half (49 per cent) of the remainder ($n = 101$) worry all or most of the time that their children will have an accident in the street. Similarly, 26 per cent of those sensitized to local dangers compared with 8 per cent of those who are not, worry about their children's risks of accidents at school. Overall, it seems that parents experience high levels of anxiety if they believe that the higher than average accident rate in their locality is a product of problems associated with the design, layout and condition of their homes and environment.

The evidence from Corkerhill is, therefore, that anxiety about accidents has tangible origins and that it cannot be seen as unreasonable or irrational. In contrast to anxiety about crime, worry about accidents – whether it relates to children at home, in the street or at school – is not loosely associated with a wide range of urban incivilities (such as petty vandalism, youths hanging about on street corners and other indirect indicators of risk). People's fears are not fuelled either by tales of local accidents: perceptions of risk are not enhanced merely by knowing people whose children have had an accident, or by simply seeing children doing 'dangerous' things. Rather, worry about accidents is directly related to parents' estimates of risk. So if parents think that their children are likely to be involved in a fall or a near miss on the road within the next month, they have an above average likelihood (20–30 per cent above average) of feeling anxious. And the risks they worry about are located in the living environment itself, not in concern about parents' attitudes, any lack of knowledge or education, or problems of time management (none of these latter variables is related to anxiety about accidents).

Anxiety about accidents is, in short, widespread, but it is not abstract or irrational. It is linked to the presence of a range of tangible risk factors which local experience has shown can rapidly be translated into serious accident events. The literature on fear of crime suggests that anxiety is heightened when people lack the resources or opportunities to control the uncertainties associated with high levels of risk (Smith 1987), and there is an extent to which this is true for fear of accidents too.

Interestingly, the problem of anxiety in Corkerhill at the moment is not any lack of informal resources or support. Lack of support networks for coping with risk are sometimes identified as an important cause of urban anxiety. However, in Corkerhill there is no relationship between worry and, for instance, the availability of informal childcare. This is probably because there is no real shortage of informal support networks in Corkerhill. We found, in fact, that an important part of the organization of safe-keeping and caring regimes depends on developing and sustaining a network of relationships with kin and others. One of the routines that parents set up as a safe-keeping strategy involves the reciprocal giving and receiving of favours with family and friends. Half the parents we interviewed had family living in the area and fewer than one in three said there is no one with whom they exchange small favours. When we asked, 'If someone told you now that you have an urgent appointment this afternoon is there someone you could leave the children with?', 83 per cent of respondents said yes. This was most likely to be their mother (32 per cent), then a neighbour (12 per cent), friend (8 per cent) or father, sister, mother-in-law or spouse (all 5 per cent).

It may be because informal caring networks are so widespread that anxiety about accidents in Corkerhill is not even higher than it is. But given the extent to which these networks are developed, it is especially disturbing that even with them levels of anxiety are high. One reason, we suspect, is that the sources of danger are generally perceived to be outside the control of local residents. 'See the workmen – they're a big danger in here because they just don't give a damn . . . Yer workmen are a lot to blame for accidents in here.' The only real control people have is over what to do and who to contact once an accident has happened. Thus ownership of a telephone – a key means of securing assistance in the formal sphere – is associated with lower than average levels of anxiety: 43/104 (41 per cent) of those with a phone compared with 54/105 (51 per cent) of those without worry all the time that their children are at risk of an accident when they are outside the home. This suggests that worries may be heightened where parents feel they have no direct recourse to assistance or to emergency services.

Experience in Corkerhill suggests that in this kind of locality, anxiety about accidents is a product of experiencing accidents, and of being aware of the prevalence of risk factors in the local environment. Anxiety is related to the trauma of having a child involved in an accident event, and to the problem of living in a high risk environment when there is no obvious way to control or deal with those risks.

The effects of anxiety

Much of the literature on urban anxiety presumes that in moderation it engenders positive preventive behaviour. The temptation therefore is to use publicity campaigns and educational initiatives to enhance people's awareness of the risks on the assumption that this will encourage them to employ avoidance strategies. This is a basic premiss of the health education approach to accident prevention. However, as we have already noted, worry and anxiety about accidents are not the same kind of emotion as a healthy awareness of risks. During the in-depth individual and group interviews we found evidence to suggest that while, theoretically, worry (because it is linked to direct experience of accidents and awareness of risks) may inform successful prevention strategies, in practice, worry and anxiety have some rather more sobering consequences.

First, parents' comments suggest that anxiety can undermine some attempts to keep children safe; second, we found that constant worry for the well-being of children can impinge on people's sense of enjoyment of, or satisfaction with, local life and the local environment; finally, there is evidence that anxiety about accident risks can undermine parents' self-esteem and affect their coping strategies. We discuss each of these effects of anxiety in turn.

Anxiety and safe-keeping

Our study suggests that those who worry most find it least easy to keep their children safe. Among those (73/209, 34 per cent) who worry most or all of the time about domestic accidents, nearly two-thirds (61 per cent) say they find it difficult, in practice, to protect their children from risk. And those who find it difficult to keep their children safe at home also worry more about other kinds of accident risks (especially accidents at school). Clearly, then, worry is not a prelude to prevention; rather, it is an emotion that tends to be enhanced by inadequate opportunities to engage in preventive behaviour. Indeed, given the disabling effects of worry, it is not surprising to find that some parents adopt what can appear to be a fatalistic outlook on accidents. Avoiding worry in this way is a coping strategy that in practice (because it is an attitude of mind, rather than a complacency in behaviour) has a positive outcome for child safety.

The extent to which people who are anxious find it hard to keep their children safe was confirmed by participants in the group interviews.

> In order to keep the kids safe you've got them trapped in the house, you're trapped in the house, you're under more pressure and that in itself is the cause of accidents. If you're goin' about there like this up tae here wi it y're no watching your kids [and] in that space of time something happens.

> When he is in the house he is trapped inside the house and that obviously greatly increases the risks inside the house.

> You can get really depressed and think about all the things [safety equipment] that your children should have . . . and add that to all the other stresses you've got – living in bad housing or poverty and you can get depressed and distracted and that's when accidents are more likely to happen.

> When you are like that – in that state [stressed] – you're no attentive tae your kids aw the time.

These impressions reflect the findings of Brown and Harris (1978), whose work in south London showed how many women had got to the stage where they lacked the means to resolve setbacks in their domestic lives and were unable to provide constant vigilance and protection. So while awareness of risks may help to inform accident prevention, anxiety may undermine the effectiveness of this, enhancing people's feelings that they have a hopeless task and cannot hope to succeed. As one parent put it,

> It seems as if there's no a happy medium. You either let them out and you're careless, or you keep them in and you're over-protective, and your lad's gonnae have an accident because you cannae teach it to be street-wise if you've got him in the house.

Parents who feel they lack the time they need to keep their children safe in a risky environment experience exceptionally high levels of stress. They are 2.5 times more likely to be anxious than those who do have sufficient time in their daily round to take the precautions they feel are required. People who worry a lot also tend to think that their children have many more near misses than they actually know about. Of those who say they worry all the time when their children are in the street, for instance, 63 per cent (61/96) think their children have lots of near misses that they never report to their parents. Of those who rarely or never worry, the comparable figure is just 45 per cent (18/40). Those who worry most may be right, but they may also be worrying needlessly and – more importantly – counter-productively.

Worry is a product of knowing the risks but feeling powerless to overcome them. It is damaging because of the extent to which the responsibilities for accidents are individualized – because those with the power to do something to help rarely acknowledge the extent to which child safety is a social value, not simply a preoccupation for parents.

Fear of accidents and residential satisfaction

High levels of concern about accidents also appear to be associated with negative views of the home and neighbourhood. The evidence we collected suggests that, because of this, fear and anxiety about accidents not only compromises individuals' safe-keeping strategies but may also undermine collective efforts to protect children from risk.

While few parents believe that Corkerhill is a *safe* place for children, those who think it is very unsafe are disproportionately likely to feel that things generally are changing for the worse. Over three-quarters (77 per cent) of those who worry all or most of the time about their children's risks of accidents in the home, but fewer than two-thirds (61 per cent) of other parents, think the locality is going downhill. The same tendency to feel that there have been changes for the worse which affect the quality of life is found among 81 per cent of those who worry about accidents in the street and among 80 per cent of those who worry about accidents at school (among those who are less anxious, 53 per cent and 77 per cent respectively feel their locality is changing for the worse). Similarly, 87 per cent (137/158) of those who regard the area as very unsafe, in contrast to 69 per cent of other parents, rate the local housing environment as below average. Moreover, nearly two-thirds (63 per cent, 46/73) of people who feel their children are at risk all the time (at home) have negative feelings about their own home, compared with just over two-fifths (42 per cent, 42/100) of those who believe their children are rarely, if ever, at risk in the domestic setting.

Feelings about the home are also negatively shaped by worry about accidents in the street. Of those who worry most or all of the time about their children's safety outside, 61 per cent (78/128) have negative feelings towards their home. Only 31 per cent (13/42) of those who never worry have the same kind of reaction. Likewise, 65 per cent (94/144) of those who have negative feelings towards their neighbourhood worry all or most of the time about safety in the street, compared with just 56 per cent (18/32) of the remainder.

When parents are anxious about accident risks, they are likely to become locked into a negative view of the whole of their living environment. The safety and well being of children are a primary focus of family life, and when the everyday spaces of household activity are shot through with danger, they impinge on virtually every other aspect of the local quality of life. Negative views about neighbourhood life and perception of neighbourhood decline have been shown in a variety of studies to undermine collective efforts by local people to manage local problems. Corkerhill is distinctive in its local activism, but there is a danger that this could be compromised if effective strategies for managing anxiety are not developed. It is clear from what parents told us that such measures would involve tackling the source of the anxiety – the risk of accidents – not adjusting the attitudes of parents or 'educating' them.

Accidents and a sense of self

Knowledge about accidents and awareness of risk is widespread in a community like Corkerhill and, as we show elsewhere, this forms a valuable store of information which could be harnessed to policies for preventing accidents and promoting safety. However, for some parents – especially in a context where practical help in accident prevention is limited – worry and anxiety may impact negatively on behaviour patterns and on assessments of self-esteem.

Those who worry most about the extent of local risk see their daily routines as fraught with difficulty. Well over half those who regard Corkerhill as very unsafe for children (89/157, 57 per cent), compared with only a third of others (18/41, 35 per cent) find this a problem in going about their daily tasks. Overall, moreover, nearly three-quarters of parents (154/209, 74 per cent) see local dangers as a problem for their household routines. 'You carry them about because you've no got a safe place to put them doon. Ah've seen me in the kitchen making something an' he's in the baby walker and I'm here and ah've got ma foot inside the baby walker so he cannae move.'

Researchers have for some time observed that anxiety about crime and perceptions of 'stranger-danger' can restrict adults' and children's activity spaces and inhibit their daily routines. In practice, children are more at risk from accidents than from abduction, and are more likely to be injured by an incivil environment than by an abusive relative. Although accidents seem less menacing, appear less newsworthy and attract less moral outrage than victimization and child abuse, it is hardly surprising that parents who worry about accident risks too often need to restrict their children's, as well as their own, freedoms.

Many parents exclude their children from parts of the house, especially the kitchen, and restrict them to other places, like the verandas (which are themselves often found to be dangerous spaces). 'When we lived round the corner, they never got out, we just kept them on the veranda . . . they stayed on the veranda and didn't go downstairs.' The point is that, often, keeping them indoors is the only way to be able to keep an eye on them, in a context where 'I learned very quickly that you don't leave a child even for a second.' Many parents try to keep their children safe by keeping them indoors for as long as possible and for certain times in the day, week and year. Under-fives in particular tend to be restricted to the house, especially in the winter, when one in three sets of parents keeps youngsters home.

> The girl two up, she was terrified to let her kids out.

> I can't imagine what kind of age I would be happy to let him outside to play. I think Alison was eight when we came here and I was very reluctant to allow her out at that stage . . . the idea of letting Steven out to play at five or six just seems horrifying.

> In the winter you tend to keep them in . . . you cannae go out with them all the time. You've got other things to do.

> For a couple of weeks after it [an accident] he wasn't allowed out.

> I keep my door snibbed when they are playing in the hall in case they wander out the front door. As for windows, I always make sure they are shut right.

More than one parent voiced concerns about the consequences of this re-strictive strategy for their children's well-being.

> His outdoor play is if and when his dad and myself are able to take him out . . . It is a tremendous worry how you are going to let him develop normally [but] the idea of letting him out to play at five or six just seems horrifying.

> She didn't want to let him out, so he was under her feet all the time. It wasn't fair to him . . . he was crying all the time to get out . . . So, she is trying to keep him safe, but there is a conflict.

> I came home from work and he is sitting with his face tripping him because she is not letting him out.

Even the teenagers we interviewed about child safety think that contain-ment in the home is the best way to ensure that youngsters are kept safe. As they pointed out when discussing their own role as carers to a hypothetical five-year-old, 'Wi' guys flyin' up and doon wi' cars an' a' that ye cannae exactly let them run aboot.' In view of the overgrown greens and limited play space provided within the Corkerhill estate, the teenagers decided that if they were in charge, the best policy would be to keep young children indoors to watch television.

Some youngsters even adopt this policy of containment for themselves: 'He won't go out, he's just frightened . . . people are too rough for him and he can't get used to it' (mother's report on son's response to an accident). Many children, if not kept within the confines of the home, are required by their parents to stay very close to the home, in the garden, the back courts, the veranda or the street in front of the dwelling.

> I wouldn't let her go out of my sight. If I don't hear her in the back . . . I'll go and look for her.

> Ma two don't get oot unless ah can let them oot in ma Ma's garden.

> You have to be a bit cautious or totally over-cautious. I am sure we are totally over-cautious.

When children are allowed out, their activity space is often restricted by protective behaviour on the part of accompanying parents or by prohibitions imposed as part of the 'rules' of being allowed out (not all of which, of course, are conscientiously observed). 'It got to the stage that I wouldn't let her down to walk; I would carry her everywhere . . . rather than letting her walk which would be what she would enjoy doing.'

Prohibitions are the commonest strategy for older children. So, for instance, only a few five- to nine-year-olds are allowed to cross the busy main road to the sports field, go to the park in the summer or play behind the local shops. The majority play close to home, where they can be observed by parents, and are always inside or close to their homes in winter. Older children – 10- to 14-year-olds – have a somewhat wider range of play places, including the neighbourhood hall, the football pitch, and the nearby Pollock estate (the area of parkland housing the Burrell art collection which backs on to Corkerhill), but like the younger children they face restrictions in winter.

Parents do recognize that they need to let their children have some freedom:

> I do worry, but at eight and a half you've got to have some sort of independence.

> If you had to worry all the time like that, every time he went out to play football, you would be just as well to take his leg off him.

Nevertheless, a substantial number of parents are not at all sure that the places their children go to are safe, and prefer to keep them as close as they can for as long as is feasible, with far-reaching consequences for their own lifestyle and routines. We asked parents when they had last had a night out without their children, and 18 per cent said they couldn't remember, while 29 per cent said it was over a month before. And within the home, safety routines displace, or at least compete for space and time, with most other responsibilities:

If you are watching Steven you are watching Steven; you can't be watching him and getting on with something else because there are so many ways that he could be hurt.

When they were young I never ironed in the day. Cause you know the phone could hae went or the door could hae went. You had to leave the iron . . . so I ironed at night.

Even with curtailed routines, constant vigilance and a range of safe-keeping strategies constantly in place, many parents faced with an acute awareness of risks, and a demonstrable inability to do much about them, experience guilt and blame themselves for not averting accidents or helping their children avoid injury.

I blame myself because I should have been more careful.

You feel it is your fault . . . you should have been more conscious of it happening.

It was maybe my own fault.

Some of this seems to rub off on the children.

I think the boys felt a little bit guilty even though they are really small themselves. I mean because she is the youngest they tend to think 'now mummy says you watch your little sister.' So if something happens they feel they should have been watching her.

She [sister of injured child] was worried about him as well. She felt it was her fault because she was playing with him at the time.

Anxiety about accidents is one response to the dangers children face in a high accident risk environment. While fear and anxiety undoubtedly generate the motivation to keep children safe, they do not provide the services and resources required to do so. Ironically, the consequence may be that fearful parents are traumatized by their seeming inability to keep their children safe, feel dissatisfied with the local environment, lose their sense of a stake in community life and find they have fewer and fewer effective coping strategies as a consequence. The effects of anxiety clearly reach far beyond the effects of accident events and beyond the harm and injury directly associated with them.

Conclusion

To summarize, one effect of a high local accident rate is to fuel anxiety about accidents. Anxiety is more than just a healthy awareness of risks, and seems likely to undermine rather than enhance accident prevention strategies, as well as to compound the stresses associated with low incomes, little power and inflexible bureaucracies. The evidence discussed in this chapter is further testimony that child accidents should not be quantified only in terms of their injury-inducing effects, and should not be costed solely as a health service expense. Accidents – injurious or otherwise – near accidents and potential accidents have social and psychological and well as physical and financial consequences. Moreover, whether or not an accident actually happens, and whether or not it actually causes an injury, may be much less significant for assessing these wider consequences than parents' belief that, given the environmental context, there is a real risk of their child being harmed.

Most of the literature on urban anxiety has been constructed with reference to studies of the effects of crime. Fear of crime, like anxiety about accidents, undermines social well-being and constrains activity space. Fear of crime has been identified as a policy problem in its own right, partly related to the risks of victimization but linked as well with many other aspects of local life and culture. Responses to fear of crime have therefore been two-pronged, seeking to tackle both the crime rate and the local origins of fear. Anxiety about accidents appears to be a different kind of sentiment, much more firmly rooted in known risks and personal experiences, and more reliably informed by local knowledge about the character of accident risks and the extent of accidents. Nevertheless, anxiety can undermine rather than enhance accident prevention by encouraging isolation and imposing restrictions on the preferred behaviours of both adults and children. There is a case, therefore, for considering how best to alleviate anxiety about accidents as well as developing more practical strategies for minimizing risk. This broad area of prevention is the subject we turn to next.

5

Keeping
children safe

Children in Corkerhill, and in neighbourhoods like it, have a higher than average risk of experiencing an accident. This is reflected in the higher than average serious accident rate in the area and in the higher than average rate of hospital admissions for injuries caused by accident events. However, areas like Corkerhill also contain – by virtue of their design and condition, and as a consequence of how they are managed and treated by outside agencies – a disproportionate concentration of accident risks. Politicians, policy-makers and many practitioners have a fairly clear idea of how they think these accidents could be managed, but as we show in this chapter, so do the parents who spend every day of the year keeping local children safe. At the moment, these two sets of views – professional and parental – do not always coincide. In this chapter, therefore, we consider them separately, before making some suggestions on how they might be reconciled.

Accident prevention: the official view

In one sense the inclusion of accident prevention as a target in the government's current strategy for the health of the nation marks a welcome recognition of a much-neglected problem. At last, accidents are squarely on the public agenda, and there is a firm commitment to making measurable progress in reducing them in the short term. Yet, despite the importance attached to achieving this goal, the pathway to it is not, it seems, open to negotiation. Instead accident prevention is part of the new drive towards health promotion, and health promotion is essentially about information, education and behavioural change. The management of accident risks is thus seen in the same way as the prevention of heart disease and AIDS, as an aspect of healthy living. Although the White Paper *The Health of the Nation* recognizes that accident prevention is a shared responsibility between national and local governments, voluntary and corporate organizations, and individuals and their families, the priorities for accident prevention will, in official eyes, 'rely primarily on information and education and will avoid the imposition of unnecessary regulations on business and individuals' (HMSO 1992: 106).

The idea is that education is the key to behavioural change, which is in turn the route to safer children. This line of reasoning was evident in the discussions we had with a group of professionals – a health visitor, two health promotion officers, a police sergeant, a representative of the housing department, a fire prevention officer and a road safety officer – working in the Corkerhill area. A number of points arising from this group interview are worth noting.

First, professionals hold a rather narrower conception of what accidents are than do parents. They view them almost exclusively as injury-producing events, and as *incidents produced by people* rather than things. 'We've got a saying in the fire brigade that there's only three causes of fires and generally it's men, women and children, and that's the sad fact of it.' 'People come home pretty drunk and the chip pan goes up.' Parents, as we have seen in Chapter 2, more readily appreciate the risks embedded in the design, quality and characteristics of the environment, while professionals see the problem as stemming from how local people interact with that environment. Thus, whereas parents frequently describe accident risks in terms of specific environmental hazards, professionals describe them in terms of the *characteristics of the children at risk*. As a consequence, some of the risks most feared by parents tend to be down-played by professionals.

> I think the parents perceive that their road is actually very bad. But that's a perception of course . . . There is a general perception that the cars are travelling faster than they actually are . . . If you look at the roads and the amount they are used and the complexity of them, they're not really that dangerous.

The problem, it seems, lies with the people interacting with the road.

> Usually it's a kid diving out on the road, a screech of brakes and it's just your luck how fast you're going . . . A number of under-fives were getting knocked down and what it seemed to be was that they tag along with an older group of children and the older group crosses and leaves these wee ones behind. And, of course, it's just too busy a road for them to cope with . . . You get people stuck in the middle. Although there is a crossing, people don't use it.

Professionals 'on the ground' thus tend to reflect the ideas held by government and built into public policy that accidents are generally produced by those involved in them, and that this is the point at which risks can be reduced.

Second, it follows that while professionals (like parents) see themselves as having a responsibility for maintaining child safety, they see this responsibility almost entirely as *a mandate to educate parents* and the children in their care. This is partly because they see other strategies as unfeasible. 'The house is there and there's no money to change it.' 'We look at family composition in terms of nuisance and everything else, but we don't look at the insides because there just isn't the money.' Additionally, the professionals genuinely see deficiencies in parental knowledge and behaviour as the core of the problem.

> There's a social thing that we have to address at some time. So we have to educate them [to see] that the home is really about the most unsafe place you can be . . . The idea of trying to supply a house with all these things is fine, but it's trying to encourage people to use them . . . We're in the business of trying to raise awareness . . . we're sort of in the game of trying to encourage people to change their views . . . you're trying to encourage people to change what they do in a home.

As a consequence, when they were asked about the development of accident prevention strategies, while parents (as we shall see) focused on wide-ranging environmental change, professionals were much more modest in ambition and focused almost solely on educational initiatives. Well guarded chip pans and tepid water, videos and teaching packages provide the key to safe neighbourhoods. So if there was an unlimited amount of money available, the professionals would use it to develop training opportunities and packages: 'On-going videos, and displays and this type of thing.' 'We're talking about behaviour and talking about having a safe place to be and also the education right through.' And if the professionals had only enough money to target one or two things? 'I would go for educating parents.' 'I would go for paid instructors for training child pedestrian skills and training in cycling skills.'

Although there was some understanding of the difficult situation that the parents face, there was also a feeling that many parents are oblivious to risk and that somehow it is their behaviour (even in relation to the use of safety equipment) that needs to be changed. Comments that met with murmurs of agreement in the professionals' group were:

> Even if we had all the money to put right all these things, put smoke alarms in and covers on plugs, etc. I think there's quite a lot of education needs to be done as well.

> I he problem . . . is that just providing safety equipment for the home doesn't mean it will get used and used properly if the parents don't see it as a particular priority . . . [if they] don't, you know, perceive or see their children as being at risk.

The problem with this line of reasoning is that, as our survey and interviews show, parents on the whole are only too aware of the risks, and often see their inability to afford safety equipment as a barrier to keeping their children safe. The professionals, in contrast, think the problem is one of competing priorities in the face of ignorance about the costs and benefits of safety strategies. As one professional observed,

> Smoke detectors should show a drastic improvement in fire-related deaths and accidents . . . it is just trying to get the message across . . . [a] three to four pound outlay from your pocket is still substantial . . . when you don't see the benefits, the benefits are hidden. You may only use it once in your life. You may never use it at all. So there's an education point of view.

In the next section, we argue that, contrary to the assumptions underlying public policy and professional opinion, many parents are well aware of the location of the most unsafe places and situations their children can be in. We therefore ask the question, if parents have already taught themselves about risk awareness and safety behaviour, where does this leave health promotion, and what does it mean for the development of effective accident prevention strategies?

Accident prevention and local knowledge

Although policy-makers and practitioners remain steeped in the health education model of accident prevention, *The Health of the Nation* does recognize the importance of setting local targets and, by implication, using local resources to tackle the problem. Our study was designed precisely to explore local knowledge about accidents, and to harness local expertise to accident prevention policy. The high prevalence of near accidents, for instance, already indicates that many potentially serious accidents are ameliorated by parents' speedy intervention, that at least one in five potential accidents is averted before it becomes dangerous, and that many potential accidents are avoided altogether by parents' imaginative and resourceful safety routines. When, moreover, we approach the problem by asking why in such a risky area there are so few serious accidents, and how parents manage to keep most of their children safe for most of the time, we begin to chart a local view on accident risks and prevention that challenges the presuppositions of the current policy environment.

As we have shown, parents in Corkerhill have a broad view of what accidents are, and this enables them to entertain a wider range of preventive options than policy-makers currently allow. They do not, we have suggested, hold the fatalistic view of accidents that much of the health promotion movement takes as its starting point. They do not believe that accidents 'just happen'. Indeed, they are acutely aware that most accidents are not accidents at all: they are all too predictable. If luck is involved in dealing with accidents, it is not so much the bad luck of encountering an accident risk as the good luck of having the foresight and opportunity to prevent unavoidable risks leading to injury or death.

Our discussion of parental ideas about accident prevention falls into three subsections. First, we show what parents do to minimize the impact of accidents they cannot avert; next we consider how they prevent near accidents turning into real accident events; finally, we assess the effectiveness of strategies adopted to avoid accidents altogether – strategies that aim to remove risks to ensure that they do not have the potential to become accident events at all.

Preventing minor accidents becoming serious

Where children are allowed some freedom to explore their worlds, and especially in environments littered with risk, some accidents are bound to occur. Parents often resign themselves to the inevitability of minor scrapes, which might be seen as an important part of the toddler's learning process. All children ask themselves questions like 'Can I get up this step?', 'Can I get out of my cot?', 'What happens if I do this?' However, careful supervision, quick thinking and appropriate interventions can prevent the minor accidents that result from these explorations becoming serious. Given that the majority of child accidents are minor, it might be assumed that parents achieve considerable success in containing the risks their children face. This is borne out in our survey, which uncovered relatively few major accidents in a context that both we and local parents judge to be extremely hazardous to children.

As Chapter 4 shows, when we asked people how often their children were at risk of serious accidental injury at home, at school or nursery and in the street (that is, an injury serious enough to require a trip to the local accident and emergency department), we discovered that only about a half of the parents think that their child is never at serious risk of an accident in the home, about a quarter feel that their child is never at risk of a serious accident in the street and just over a third thought that their child was never at risk at school. Parents know that accidents are a hazard and that there is safekeeping to do.

Furthermore, over 37 per cent of parents find it impossible, very difficult or quite difficult to keep their children safe at home, given the environment in which they live and the range of responsibilities they have to discharge. Keeping their children safe from the risk of accidents in the street is felt by nearly 19 per cent of parents to be impossible, and by a further 57 per cent to be very difficult or quite difficult. It is only at school or nursery that nearly half the parents feel it is quite or very easy to keep children safe (but many others clearly do not share this view). These difficulties are reflected in parental expectations about the likelihood of their children experiencing an accident over the next month. Nearly a third of parents think that during this time their children are 'certain' to fall over and graze their elbows or knees and a further 48 per cent say that eventuality is very likely or quite likely. Likewise, 43 per cent of parents think their children are certain, very likely or quite likely to have a narrow escape on the road in the next month.

The point is that, given this degree of felt risk, the relatively low numbers of accidents reported in our accident 'census' indicate to us that parents and children are being pretty successful most of the time in containing most of the risks they encounter. Indeed, parents are generally confident of their ability to protect their children from serious injury related, for instance, to burns or scalds: 92 per cent feel their children are unlikely or certain not to sustain such injuries in the near future. Some indication of how parents manage to prevent minor accidents turning into more serious injury-producing events is contained in the interview data.

Most obviously, in virtually all the accidents we discussed (with the exception of those associated with activities supervised by other responsible adults, such as football), the parents were nearby. When a young girl got caught in barbed wire left hanging by workmen at the front of one tenant's veranda, her cries immediately alerted both parents (as well as the workmen) to the danger. Her father, who had anyway been popping out from time to time to keep an eye on her, reached her first. He was able to minimize the damage to his daughter's face and to ensure that she received immediate medical attention. Likewise, when another youngster broke her wrist trying to walk down three steps in her roller boots, both parents were immediately on the scene and were able to arrange to get her to hospital. When a third child was bitten by a dog, her mum was beside her almost quickly enough to catch the animal concerned.

It is easy to argue that had the children been supervised constantly, some of these events would have been averted, rather than having their effects contained. This, however, underestimates the difficulty of integrating safety into all the other essential household routines. For instance, one mum put her children in the bedroom to play while she cooked a meal. As she pointed out,

You can't watch them when you are in the kitchen – well obviously you don't want little children in the kitchen when you are cooking anyway. It is a bit dangerous, and they played well, that's the idea, so they can play in the room where they are safe.

The accident that followed (a daughter falling from a bunk bed and break-ing her leg) resulted directly from a mother's attempts to keep her children relatively safe while attending to other basic household needs. It was at least the second potentially serious accident in the same setting (the same child had previously broken a leg by falling from a wardrobe), but the mum could not think of any alternative safe-keeping strategy.

It is either that or you let them go out and play in the street, because they obviously can't play in the back yards, because that is where the bins and everything are, and they are not very nice back yards anyway: they are full of muck and dog dirt and, I mean, they are filthy. And then there is the swing park which is quite a little bit away, and they are more likely to have an accident there than anywhere else.

Furthermore, even where parents are present, it is often hard to anticipate that an accident might arise from behaviour that has perhaps been a feature of daily life for months. Archie and his sister, for instance, were spending a normal evening: 'they were both in good moods, high spirited, just playing, carrying on and jumping on top of each other.' Their mother was there too, and completely helpless to prevent Archie's wrist being broken against a piece of wood forming part of the couch in the rough and tumble. What she could do was apply basic first aid and call a taxi to take her son to hospital. Subsequently, she also replaced the offending settee with a softer piece of furniture.

Similarly, Shona's mum was taking a normal route home on a quiet evening, when they came across rubble on the pavement. Because of this, she took Shona's hand. 'She was still holding my hand when she fell, but when she fell she fell flat on her face on to this rubble.' An appropriate preventive strategy had been introduced to modify a normal routine, but the character of the risk meant that it was not sufficient to prevent an accident occurring.

Where parents may be more at a loss is when their normal routines are disrupted; for instance around Christmas. It was two days before Christmas when Billy's mum left her son for a moment in a draining bath while she went to get a towel which was warming by the fire in another room. For the first time in his life, Billy managed while she was out to turn on a tap – the hot one, which, in common with those in 86 per cent of estate homes, is not controlled by a thermostat. After pouring some cold water on to his burned leg, 'I totally panicked and just dragged him through to the living room, but

I knew not to put the towel near it or anything like that.' She nevertheless phoned a taxi, took him to hospital and implemented sufficient safe-keeping strategies to contain the damage.

There are some accidents that parents simply cannot intervene in, especially those related to sports injuries. However, the interview data reveal a high level of responsibility in dealing with the aftermath of these. One mum is used to her son returning home with football injuries, keeps a first aid kit especially to deal with this and sees herself as a good first-aider for the kind of injuries he is likely to sustain (although the knowledge is the type 'just picked up over the years' rather than gained from formal training).

Of course, parents are limited financially and bureaucratically in what they can achieve in the long term, and this is a cause of some distress. One mum ran through a catalogue of preventable danger threatening her toddler:

> The garden is dangerous because they ripped out my hedge and put a metal fence up . . . a hedge might have taken his eye out, but a metal fence could kill him, it could crack his skull. That annoys me, it angers me. It angers me that they won't do anything about the thermostat, even though I said Billy had an accident.

She went on to say that her solicitor is arguing that she is technically homeless because her dwelling is so dangerous for her and her son, who is in any case disabled.

Similarly, a number of accidents in Corkerhill appear to have been precipitated by building and roadworks. Gordon, for instance, broke two bones in his arm by falling from scaffolding on a neighbouring house. His mother argued that it should probably not have been left up in the first place, but if it had to be there, she pointed out, some means of discouraging children from climbing on it should at least have been attempted.

> With the amount of scaffolding in this scheme, you would think they would have a watchman of some description . . . I don't think they should have left it [scaffolding]. If they had to leave it, they should have prepared it for the kids not to get at it, but I suppose it's easier said than done.

While one might well ask what Gordon was doing up the scaffolding anyway, this has to be set in the context of a community with few diversions for children and young people, and nothing on site:

> There is not the right amenities for them, and during the summer, they normally like to go down to Bellahouston Sports Centre, you know how they have the summer sports. But then again, that is expensive. It is £1.30. It is £1.30 to get in, and that is not including their bus fares if we don't walk.

In conclusion, there is evidence that when accidents do occur, not only do parents intervene to contain the physical and psychological injury that may result from them, but they also have a number of reasonable ideas about what causes accidents to happen and how they might be prevented in the future.

Preventing near accidents actually happening

One-tenth of parents know of local children other than their own who have had a serious accident at home or at school. Two-fifths of parents know of serious child accidents on the local roads. Of the 16 who thought the home accidents could have been prevented, seven said this could have been achieved by better supervision of the children; the remainder said physical changes such as cupboard locks or stair guards were needed. Of the nine who thought the school accidents could have been prevented, seven thought better supervision was the answer. Of the 77 who thought the street accidents could have been prevented, 36 (47 per cent) linked prevention to the imposition of controls on traffic, while 14 (18 per cent) again mentioned supervision of the children.

In so far as local accidents are thought of as preventable, then, parents do see their own behavioural strategies as important. Indeed, 40 per cent of respondents agree that accidents often happen when parents aren't careful enough. Given this high level of awareness of parental responsibility, parental intervention is one of the key features associated with the aversion of accidents – a process in which Corkerhill's parents have proved exceedingly successful, despite the disproportionately wide range of risks that require their vigilance.

We collected interview data on 12 near accidents. Five were incidents involving traffic, two each centred on electric sockets and dangerous windows, and the remaining incidents involved a baby walker and some steps, a veranda and an unguarded fire. It is common practice in areas like anaesthesia and aeronautics – where most people are safe most of the time, but where even a small mistake can have tragic consequences – to examine things that nearly go wrong to find clues about how to minimize future risks. Accident studies, preoccupied as they are with injury and mortality, rarely examine events that *nearly* occur. Yet these are in some ways the success stories – the moments when a potential disaster is, by a mixture of good training, good practice, good discipline and good luck, avoided.

Discussions of the near accidents on the roads revealed a number of points. First, parents spend a lot of time telling their children how to cross the road safely, but children are unpredictable and drivers need to be aware of this. Drivers' vigilance is at least as crucial as parental alertness in averting road accidents in residential neighbourhoods, where design features are not geared to the separation of people and traffic.

There were cars going about all the time, and children playing. It was very busy – cars parked at the closes and things like that. People were walking about . . . it was a nice night . . . The two of them [aged 8 and 5] just ran out of the close and never looked right or left or anything – just went straight out . . . They would normally look to see where they were going. I don't know what was wrong with them that day. The two of them ran in front of a car and it stopped but nearly hit them. I was screaming down the stairs to tell them to watch what they were doing.

She just came running down and ran on to the road although I told her to wait. She went in between two cars and the car had actually to brake to miss her . . . She knows better but she still goes out and does it . . . The other day . . . she ran out again and I checked her for it and I just turned my back and she did exactly the same thing. All you can do is keep your eyes on them but you can't do that 24 hours a day.

Second, drivers routinely speed and often ignore pedestrian lights.

There was the green man and my husband, and the pavement was there [illustrates with arm movements], and my husband and this friend of mine were about like that [illustrates position], and he started to cross, and this driver came . . . it was a motor cycle, and he never stopped, and he just missed.

The cars are coming up and down all the time and there are taxis, they come up and down like nobody's business, they go too fast, and the kids are playing on their bikes and that, and the kids don't have a chance.

They [drivers] don't see traffic lights because they are going so fast coming up the hill and they come down so fast before they realize they have got traffic lights in front of them.

Third, the lights may fail to work. 'Sometimes these lights are not working either. These lights are always breaking down.'

Fourth, the residential and commercial zone is used in a cavalier manner by drivers. This means that adults out with children cannot relax their vigilance in what might – in a safer residential environment – be thought of as a normal way. In one incident the child concerned was in a play area, and the adult carer was nearby talking to a neighbour. The two children ran from the play area across a car park, just as a lorry (which should have been using a nearby loading bay, and a nearby lorry park) reversed into the car park and nearly hit them.

Fifth, the car parking and garaging facilities are inadequate, so that cars parked on the road create an additional hazard.

There are too many cars for the size of this scheme and nowhere to put them . . . when you have parking on both sides you can't get by . . . it is dangerous for the weans because they go in between the motors to see if another motor is coming.

Discussions relating to other near accidents show that accidents are a consequence of real, and often unnecessary, risks that parents keep under control through a combination of vigilance, quick thinking and good luck. One near accident concerned a toddler trying to plug an electric light into a live socket. One problem was that the safety cover bought by the parents had not been replaced after the socket was last used, because the parents had not realized how aware their toddler was of the existence of the socket. Another factor, however, was that they had moved to Corkerhill from a much safer dwelling.

The sockets we had in that house were on/off switches, and were not in obvious places. You know they were kind of built into fireplaces and in areas where they are not seen, so they don't get to them very easily . . . This is a different house and the situation here is very very different. We have to be a lot more aware and there are a lot more hazards living here with a baby than there were when the other two were young.

Another near accident concerned a toddler almost falling from a window, which she had accidentally opened by knocking the handle. Despite the ease of opening having been reported to the council, no changes had been made: 'I said that the windows could be easily opened and they said they didn't have the money, so they are still the same.' This was just one of many complaints referring to the dangers associated with windows and window frames. Another parent told us: 'We had about a year when the putty hadn't set in the window, so my windows – you could do that [gestures] – and the pane of glass was actually hanging out the window and that was about a year.'

Most parents felt that it was primarily good luck that prevented near accidents becoming real risks, although in almost every case there is evidence that what really happened was a consequence of quick thinking and swift action on the part of one or more adults, or of the children themselves. On one occasion, for instance, a toddler in a baby walker followed her mum to the door.

Somebody was at the door and I went to answer it, and the baby was in her baby-walker, and she came running up to the door and the baby-walker hit right off the step and it toppled but I just happened to catch her before she fell right over.

On another occasion a mother was cooking in the kitchen, leaving her nine-month-old in the safety of the living room. However, an older child had opened a door on to the veranda. 'I was at the cooker and I heard someone screaming from outside and you know that way that you just know it is one of your children . . . and I ran up to the porthole window just in time to see her lower herself under the veranda.' The neighbours' vigilance gave the mother a chance to catch the child with one arm, though in the meantime several other people had positioned themselves either to catch the child if she fell or to stop her falling at all. The attraction of windows is another potential hazard, which again is not restricted to parents who are not quite vigilant enough, or to children who are too bold. A Scottish newspaper reported on the children and windows danger:

> An angry mum told . . . how her daughter toppled 30ft from a second storey window. The fall happened as the four year old and her eight month old sister were being looked after by a social worker. Little Cheryl escaped death when she was CAUGHT by a passerby. Her furious mum . . . said: 'I only left my children for 10 minutes to go to a shop' . . . A social work spokesman said: 'The social worker who had been helping to move the mother in [to her new flat] was distracted. There is no question of the social worker being negligent.'
>
> (*Daily Record* 9 July 1992: 17)

Incidents like these arise partly because parents have to balance their domestic responsibilities in a realistic way, and cannot watch every child all the time. They arise, too, because in a risky environment it is hard to know which hazard to watch and when. As the mother involved in the veranda incident notes, 'You don't think. I never ever thought a child could squeeze through that space. It didn't cross my mind for a minute.' This accident was averted by quick thinking (rather than good luck), and it quickly became part of a pool of local learning. Many parents are acutely aware that it is this kind of situation that helps them prevent future accidents. 'Everything like this does make you a bit more cautious; a bit more aware to check things . . . That is how your safety awareness develops, by things which nearly happen, just managing to avert them.' They also point out that this learning process extends to children: 'We would tell them not to climb on the veranda and they were good that way . . . they understood and they knew about accidents because their cousin had an accident with scaffolding.'

Furthermore, while parents often want more information on some issues – safety education for their children, first aid training for themselves – the kind of practical knowledge that comes from astute conduct in a hazardous area is likely to be much more useful as a basis for prevention strategies than the kind of safety information that is currently handed down by the 'professionals'.

> You could be offered a lot of information, but it's what could you do about it? It is all right having the information, but it is still difficult to

watch little children no matter what information you have . . . Little children . . . you can't, especially when you have other little ones, watch them all the time.

Safety routines: preventing risks becoming accidents

In their day-to-day lives, the people of Corkerhill intervene as a matter of routine to keep their children's living and play space as safe as possible. For instance, living in a cold damp atmosphere constrains behaviour and increases the need for vigilance. As one mother put it in the group interview, 'Because it's cold, we eat in the living room at the coffee table, and everything's low down, the coffee, the tea. You're constantly on the alert, aren't you?'

Parents are aware that stress can be instrumental in turning risks into accidents, and that they need to take care when things prove too much.

> I've seen me going round and saying to my mother, 'Go on, take the weans,' just to get that wee bit of peace and quiet, or say to ma mammy if she's up, 'Go on, stay with them for half an hour,' and maybe just going out, you know how, just tae . . .

But in some cases there is no mother to help out. One group described the plight of a girl who had a variety of problems, including a child in hospital:

> Every time she went tae her doctor, there was Valium and stuff like that he was giving her. She ended up like a zombie. So that doesnae help anybody. How can she take care of her kids if she's doped up, and that's no through negligence on her part. That's the doctor just writing out a prescription, and she just cannae tackle things.

It was widely agreed in the group discussions that 'the doctors are inclined tae give out anti-depressants instead of trying to tackle the cause.'

Sometimes parents make physical changes to the environment to deal with the kinds of hazards they know might precipitate an accident event. In one case, for instance, a gap through which a child could crawl was blocked with a piece of wood: 'Paul caught our cat crawling under it, and he just done the same, and yet he was just playing, you know. So my boy put a bit of wood there so he couldnae get out. Ye cannae leave them, you know what I mean?' In other cases parents intervene to ensure that other people take adequate safety measures.

> A lot of the time, you've got to be really stroppy with them to get something done . . . I was going up to my mother's – going up the road there, and they had dug this hole – and it was about the length of that carpet on the pavement – no a workman in sight and it was about this deep [gestures] and I was supposed to either go over that with a pram,

or go to Braidcraft Road, where they're all doing about 50 miles per hour on a bend, with a pram, and luckily enough Fiona [older child] was there, and I just stopped the pram, and she's going 'Mum, don't embarrass me.' 'Shut up' [laughs]. I went in and I kicked up merry hell about the fact that there wasnae a board or anything put over it, and it ended up two workmen came out and lifted the pram over the hole, and then left somebody there on guard. There wasnae even a soul that you could say, 'Look, could you go out till that traffic's safe and I'll do it that way.' No, not a thing, and by the time I came back, they had a workman standing on it, they had boards across it, and by the next morning, it was all cemented. So I think that part of the things we have tae dae is be voluble – is to shout and is to say: 'C'mon, get the finger oot, it's time something was done.'

There is no shortage of information from the group and individual interviews about the ways that safety consciousness is incorporated into everyday life. When asked specifically for their views about the best way to reduce accidents in Corkerhill, parents concentrated on two kinds of suggestion: the provision of safe places for children to play and the implementation of traffic calming measures. One in every two parents mentioned one of these strategies as the first step to improving local child safety. In the absence of any provision for these in the physical infrastructure of the area, parents developed a range of informal measures designed to achieve the same preventative ends.

To deal with the traffic

Dangerous roads and careless drivers are seen by parents as the main danger to children in Corkerhill and they adopted a number of safety routines to minimize risk.

Fewer than half the parents of children aged 14 or under had access to a car or van. Most, though, could recall the last time their children had travelled in a car, van or taxi. Not surprisingly in a community where car ownership is low, for over a quarter of children their last car journey had been in a taxi. For the vast majority of children, the usual safety routines associated with motor vehicle transport had been observed. Well over 90 per cent had travelled in the back seat, and the majority had worn a seat belt where such belts were fitted.

About three-quarters of children of bike riding age had ever ridden a bike (not necessarily their own), but helmet wearing was very rare. A few more wore reflective articles or fluorescent clothing, and about twice as many wore something white, presumably in the parental hope that this would make them more visible. Interestingly, when a small payment was made to Corkerhill towards the costs of keeping the community hall heated for interviewers, and for delivering leaflets about the research, it was chosen to spend some of this on cycle helmets to be given as prizes.

The journey to and from school is a particularly dangerous time for children, with many road traffic accidents to children taking place at this time. Swedish experts do not believe that it is reasonable to expect a child to undertake the numerous perceptual, motor and other skills needed to cross the road successfully before the age of about ten. Many Corkerhill parents apparently concurred with this view – or went further. We asked, 'At what age do you think a child can walk to school on his or her own around here without being at risk from an accident?' Two people felt that children were not safe at any age, and a further 29 per cent suggested ages ranging from 11 to 16. A quarter thought that ten was about the right age to walk safely to school without risk of an accident, a further 42 per cent suggested ages between seven and nine, five parents thought six, and a couple five or four.

Most children in Corkerhill walk to school and the majority have to cross a busy road on the way. They are usually accompanied to school by their parents or by older children (although older children tend to go to school with their friends). The group interviews indicate that taking children to and from school takes a considerable chunk out of the parents' day, as there is no school actually in Corkerhill. Many children also returned home for lunch. The time this takes is a price mothers are prepared to pay.

To create safe play spaces
In order to reduce their children's exposure to risk, many parents routinely restrict their play space. One-third of parents say that it is not safe to let children under seven (boys or girls) out alone. Virtually all parents with children under ten restrict their access to some parts of the local neighbourhood, and nearly nine out of ten of those with children over ten years do the same. Over three-quarters of those with children under five, and 15 per cent of those with five- to nine-year-olds, don't allow them out to play locally at any time. Two-thirds of those with 5–14-year-olds allow them out only during the hours of daylight.

Other kinds of restrictions may also be imposed by parents. For instance, many interviewees commented on the dangers associated with roadworks and construction works associated with housing renovations and repairs. The unanimous view is that insufficient care is taken during these projects to ensure the public's safety. Following Shona's accident, which occurred as a consequence of local building works, her parents were so concerned that

> It got to the stage [where] I wouldn't let her down to walk; I would carry her everywhere. If I wasn't, my husband was, or we were taking the pram to go round to my mum's – a short distance – rather than letting her walk which would be what she would enjoy doing.

The work of Hillman *et al.* (1990) has shown how parental concerns for accidents can restrict children's mobility. Moreover, children themselves may also adopt restrictive behaviour. One mother told us 'My middle son just won't go out because – I don't know – we are not long back in this area . . . He has come back here and turned into a hermit. He just won't go out. He's frightened, he's not used to it.' Many parents also limit their own social life in order to keep an eye on their children. Nearly one in five say they can't remember the last time they went out for an evening without their children, and a further 29 per cent say it has been at least a month since they did this. Even trips for basic necessities can be curtailed, and even for mothers who have teenagers as well as toddlers. 'I would never say that I was going up to the shops and [would they, the teenagers] look after him for an hour because I don't know which one would be most likely to have an accident, him or them.'

Safety issues pervade a number of household routines, especially those associated with essential housework. In flatted and tenemental properties, hanging out the washing, for instance, is rarely a straightforward task, since it generally requires wet clothing to be carried down concrete stairways to the communal 'green' where the clothes lines are located. One-fifth of the parents we spoke to never use the greens (often encountering the displeasure of the local housing factor by hanging their clothes on their verandas). Of those ever needing to juggle the demands of washing and children, four out of five (118/142) had to find a way to transport the children and the washing at the same time, often because they could not find a safe space indoors to leave them. The majority achieved this by carrying them, holding their hand or strapping them into a buggy. Only five mothers said their husband or an older child was usually present to help them.

Safety issues also impinge on the use of the dwelling and the organization of rooms. 'Three or four times we've completely moved the furniture because, you know, if the television was in this side of the room, the sockets were completely exposed and all the plugs going into that were in nice easy reach.' In a hazardous environment like Corkerhill, there is an extent to which safety has to become a social value, and this is borne out in the way in which social networks have formed to provide a collective sense of child care responsibility. More than four in five parents in our survey said they have someone they could leave their children with if they had an urgent reason to have to go out that afternoon. Mostly this resource is either a relative (44 per cent would call on a mother or mother-in-law) or a neighbour (15 per cent would resort to a neighbour).

Parents can also rely on friends and neighbours to watch their children as a matter of routine.

I am always at the window to see they are all right, and the neighbours downstairs keep an eye on them as well . . . it's a quieter place here than round the corner, you know, and all the neighbours watch the kids and that is what I like about it.

A 'bottom-up' view of accident prevention

While policy-makers and professionals currently orientate their accident prevention strategies around education for parents and children, the evidence we have collated here suggests that the parents themselves have quite a different idea about what effective accident prevention consists of. Parents living in an unsafe environment have day-to-day experience of what puts their children at risk, and day-to-day routines designed to keep them safe. 'You're more educated than any academic because you live in it daily . . . you might no be able to use words of 42 syllables, but you *know* better.'

Parents do recognize that they have a pivotal role in maintaining child safety. In this they are in full agreement with policy-makers and professionals. However, whereas professionals currently insist that their main responsibility is to educate parents, parents insist that much more than this is needed if child safety is really on the agenda. Parents argue that the regional and district councils, the housing department, the roads department, workmen employed in the area and so on all have a responsibility for the safety of local children. At the moment, they feel no confidence that this duty is being discharged.

At worst, they feel ignored:

Ye see other areas . . . an you see the potential there fur the rent ye're paying . . . that's really so frustrating – that you can see it all happening round aboot ye, and we are jist ignored.

It's like a lost village this . . . it's beginning tae feel like a lost village.

Ah think they [the professionals] know that it's a forgotton place.

Simple [safety] gadgets could be made up, but when you're in an area like this you don't get any help. You're totally isolated an there's no much chance of anything getting better. The authorities aren't going to come in and suddenly say, 'we will put on all these safety things because child accidents are our priority.' It's great on paper and they are into all these reports an what everybody should be doin' and all the rest of it. But when it comes to the practical sides . . . that's too expensive . . . they'll talk about their priorities being children, but in real terms they are the last of their worries.

At times they feel patronized:

They've stopped slappin' us about an tellin us no to complain . . . nowadays they're fallin' over themselves with sympathy. We don't want sympathy . . . we want action . . . They say, 'aw, that's a shame, ah wouldnae like tae stay in that.' They don't actually do anything.

They talked aboot it, but nothing . . . The next month we went, they talked about it again . . . Ah think what they should do is let somebody from the council or higher up stay in one o' they houses one winter.

At best, they feel that well-meaning professionals have simply got it wrong:

Ah feel sometimes that some of the health visitors don't have a clue what they're talking about. I mean, quite honestly, because they havnae really handled a situation . . . sometimes they tell you practical stuff . . . you know, *it isn't practical.*

It's all right having the information, but it's still difficult to watch little children no matter how much information you have.

The parents asked for grass [for landscaping the backcourts]. They got pebbles. It was a daft idea anyway, pebbles. We know better. You don't want loose pebbles when you've got kids running about.

The irony is that parents not only have good ideas about creating and maintaining a safe environment, they also tend to alight on relatively simple and cost-effective ways of doing this. In our group interviews, we asked respondents to suggest cheap ways of preventing accidents. Those groups made up by residents from the community were far more imaginative, and better informed, particularly in the detail of how this would be done, than were the group of professionals. We also asked for ideas on strategies where the sky would be the limit as far as cost was concerned (this was particularly appealing to the professionals), where there was just enough funding to do one or two things and where there was no extra funding, but existing resources and services could be shifted.

Not surprisingly, people who live in poverty are rather more imaginative than professionals, who do not, in suggesting low cost strategies. Indeed, low cost preventive measures were *only* suggested by the community groups. These involved: applying rules to ensure that people carrying out repairs in the neighbourhood take safety into account; supporting community run playgroups (something which has now been put in place with the 'wee horrors' playgroup); and initiating a scheme in which the children themselves have a role in identifying local dangers, thus putting them in the position of being the 'safety police' rather than the more passive role with which children are more familiar.

Even in making proposals for high cost strategies there are some telling differences between the community and professionals' groups. Relatively high, or very high, cost proposals included: educational campaigns (professionals); knocking down the estate and starting again, or, failing that, replacing rotten window frames, providing electric sockets with on/off switches and designing safer back courts and closes (community); and providing a safe play area 'so people don't go doon and start playing chicken with the buses and things like that' (teenagers). The professionals assumed that the community needed to know about the dangers; the community knew it had enough information on what the dangers are, and made appropriate proposals to deal with them.

Lay expertise has often been derided or ignored in the past. Women, for instance, were advised not to listen to other women ('old wives' tales') about childbirth. Professional advice has tended to be portrayed as more rational than personal experience, scientific knowledge as more reliable than local wisdom. Thus parents concerned about rising rates of asthma among local children are told that it is the result of better diagnosis rather than worse health: it is because doctors are doing their jobs better, not because the housing environment is getting worse. And when parents in Corkerhill made plans for a safety equipment loan scheme, it failed because the local health promotion department was unable to provide any support, offering instead a specially commissioned – and thus not inexpensive – poster. Meanwhile, parents resorted to their imagination (such as in cutting old cots up to make safety gates or playpens) and generally harnessed the resources they did have at hand to try to create a safer environment overall.

The lesson from this is that where parents do not appear to be pursuing safe behaviours, the reason is more likely to be lack of opportunity than lack of knowledge. The work of Hilary Graham (1987, 1994) is helpful for understanding the way in which behaviours and lifestyle are constrained by material and environmental circumstances. She was concerned with why women living in very poor material circumstances tend to continue to smoke, regardless of being well informed about the risks it entails. Her studies show that although these women know they are putting their own health at risk, the practice does reduce other risks – notably the perceived risks that arise from the stress of dealing with small children while managing on a very low income. Likewise, in communities like the one we studied, the availability of funds to buy safety equipment must compete with the other financial priorities that arise from having children in the household. Other hazards supposedly amenable to containment through appropriately safe behaviours are even further beyond parental control. Fully 86 per cent of families with children in Corkerhill cannot regulate the water temperature of their boilers. With the built-in potential for scalding water to flow out of any hot tap, educational campaigns around the idea of lowering temperatures are singularly redundant, and even where they are potentially effective their impact has been slight (Katcher 1987; Webne et al. 1989). On the other hand, legislation to ensure that water temperatures are pre-set at safe levels has proved successful in reducing scald casualties (Erdmann et al. 1991).

The problem, we feel, is that so much of prevention policy is about adapting behaviours to environments, whereas when we look at the problem from the point of view of those experiencing it, it is the environment that constrains the options for implementing safety routines. Where the material or environmental constraints are lifted, safety behaviours are reliably implemented. So, for instance, while professionals cast doubt on whether people will bother to fit free smoke alarms, in the event four in every five families in a trial distribution did have them fitted and operational within a few months of receiving them (Gorman *et al.* 1985). The result of failing to recognize the extent to which safety behaviours are constrained by local circumstances is a suite of accident prevention messages which appear unrealistic to those who are expected to act on them.

How does a child cross the main road in Glasgow if she is told in her road safety sessions: 'Never cross between parked cars', 'Don't cross the road if you can see another car coming'? As in most major cities, if this advice were to be rigidly followed, youngsters would never be able to cross the road. The same goes for some of the messages to parents. It will be difficult enough for the mother living in the most privileged conditions to follow consistently the advice not to leave her children on their own. If you are a mother living three floors up in a Glasgow tenement with three under-fives, and you want to hang your washing on the green below, how do you put this advice into practice? Advice is directed far more fiercely and consistently towards children and their carers than towards planners, architects, drivers and those responsible for building sites.

Despite the wariness about local knowledge that professionals and policy-makers continue to express, Peter Pharaoh, a professor of public health, has recently described with admirable humility the importance of lay knowledge in relation to some early work he did in New Guinea:

> Here was a local well-recognized condition, endemic cretinism, which had risen sharply in prevalence within less than a decade. The local community were convinced that the disease post-dated first contact with the white man, but my arrogant assumption was that the rise in prevalence was owing to better survival and not a change in incidence. Subsequent investigations proved the local community right, and the lessons of humility and of listening to the patient, be they the individual or community, had to be learnt.
>
> (in Ashton 1994: 165)

It seems that this lesson is learnt more quickly in some contexts than in others. The causes of many industrial illnesses, for instance, have been recognized by those working with particular substances or in particular environments long before their origins have become more widely accepted. Mesothelioma is a case in point.

Despite all this, Laidman's (1987) work draws attention to a continuing lack of critical attention in the literature to parents' perspectives on safety. Our findings suggest that these perspectives are important. We suspect, further, that children's ideas would also be valuable. Children's views of risk and danger in relation to accidents are largely unexplored. There has been some work examining children's views of accidents and accident prevention in a school setting (Child Accident Prevention Trust and Roberts 1993), and work on children's perception of risks forms part of the ESRC risk initiative, but much of the current literature in this field is at the level of asking children to spot dangers from pictures. Having had their accident prevention talk, most children can fairly reliably spot the problems of trailing flexes, sharp knives and unguarded pots on the stove. Whether this can be translated into accident prevention behaviours is quite another matter. We had hoped to include this is our own study, but when our funding was cut from an already modest two years to a tightly costed one year, this more demanding and speculative part of the work had to go.

In the end, it is our contention that parents' – and, when available, children's – perspectives on accident prevention are important for at least three reasons. First, all the public policy in the world will not bring the accident rate down if the parents in the front line feel their own views are marginalized by professionals and practitioners working to a remote agenda. Second, it is unlikely that locally effective prevention policies can be formulated without recourse to the local knowledge that only local people are in a position to acquire. Finally, local people tend to come up with prevention strategies that are more cost-effective than those of bureaucrats and politicians. If local knowledge is not taken into account it seems unlikely that accident reduction targets will be met. If local expertise is harnessed by those responsible for safety campaigns, there is every possibility that effective prevention strategies could be designed even within the budgets set by a restructured public sector.

Conclusion

It is often assumed that a key factor explaining the social distribution of accidents relates to parents' safety education and sense of responsibility. Our research suggests that parents in a high risk area like Corkerhill have a strong sense of their safe-keeping responsibilities, that they have a detailed knowledge of risks, and that they have developed a range of preventive strategies on the basis of this knowledge. Where they fail to prevent or avert accidents, it is often because there are simply so few safe spaces in a place like Corkerhill, and because the challenge of keeping children safe and attending to other essential household routines is too demanding. Yet even where prevention is impossible parents are often successful in containing the damage caused by accidents. This does not mean that parents do not need help in keeping their children safe. What it means is that risks are specific to local environments, that prevention strategies are learned in these local contexts and that policies for safe-keeping must therefore be based on local knowledge.

6

Conclusion

Our aim in this book has been to use a set of case studies in a high risk area to examine the causes and consequences of child accidents and to inform accident prevention policy. Using three methods – group interviews, a household survey and a set of case studies of actual or averted accidents and near misses – we have explored the ways in which safety is managed and danger negotiated alongside the other demands of life in an uncertain environment. While much work concerned with child accidents and accident prevention is concerned with individual experiences and responsibilities, our main interest has been in what Suchman (1961) has referred to as safety as a social value.

Our key challenge, then, has been to examine the problem of child accidents in the wider social and environmental context in which they arise. To this end, we have described the part played by issues of safety and risk in the lives of those caring for children and in the routines of the children themselves. We have described the geography and sociology of accident risks, we have illustrated some ways in which parental (usually maternal) concerns about child safety are incorporated into daily routines and we have shown how these routines are shaped not only by accidents themselves but also by worry and anxiety about the magnitude of risk. We have used this information to show how parents help their children avoid or avert accident risks, and we have used it, too, to help us consider why safety routines sometimes fail, so that accidents happen.

The findings from the group interviews that marked the beginnings of our research painted a picture of a caring community, aware of dangers and motivated to tackle them. It was, after all, the community that alerted us to the problem, requested our involvement and provided the stimulus for the project to go ahead. Parents' collective ideas about danger, safety, risk and prevention provided valuable input into the prevalence survey, which formed the second stage of the research. The survey we describe in Chapter 2 thus allows for the fact that parents see accidents as just one element of life's insecurity and as one further hazard for people living in damp, cold houses, managed by a faceless bureaucracy. It acknowledges, too, that parents have a detailed knowledge of local dangers and can fairly accurately predict when and where their children will encounter them.

The survey itself allowed us to assemble a census of child accidents based not simply on injury data or on indices of health service use, but also on every kind of accident event that people experience. This yielded a more detailed picture of how, when, where and why children are at risk than anything available in official statistics. It also provided a comprehensive overview of the kinds of problem a high risk area faces, drawing attention to the wide range of dangers embedded in the environment – dangers that constrain the character and effectiveness of the safe-keeping strategies which are common among parents and, indeed, children.

Drawing on experiences reported to us during the prevalence survey, we were able to go on, in the third part of the project, to study in detail a set of accidents, near accidents and averted accidents. These qualitative case studies, conducted by specially trained interviewers, looked at the whole context of each accident or near accident, discussing what had happened before, what happened at the time and what has happened since. The richness of the interview transcripts enabled us to understand – in a way that neither routinely collected official statistics nor quantitative survey methods could ever do – the antecedents as well as the consequences of accidents. We were able by this method to get a much fuller idea of what risky places and behaviours mean.

In conducting this work, we were warmly and generously welcomed into Corkerhill, and our study there ran alongside a number of initiatives run by local residents to attempt to make the community a better and safer place to live in. Some of these have been successful. Every house now has (or has been offered) a smoke alarm, central heating is to be installed in some of the unheated houses and there is a children's group working on safety issues. People in the community have many more ideas for improving the well-being and safety of themselves and their children, and are actively trying to put them into place. During the course of our work there and since, some local people have had an opportunity to describe their work, explain their successes and reflect on their failures at meetings and conferences within and outside Glasgow. The community has become part of the WHO Safe Community Network, two members of the community, Betty Campbell and Walter Morrison, attended the International Conference on Safe Communities in Atlanta, Georgia, and Cathie Rice is now involved in community safety on a full-time basis, as an officer for the nearby Safe Pollock initiative.

Our work was not, then, a piece of action research. There was plenty of action already happening and our involvement was not designed to intervene in this process. What it was designed to do was to explore people's experiences of accidents in a way that only intense case study research can, in order to shed new light on the neglected problem of child accident risks. The kind of data we collated enabled us to consider just what lies at the heart of the child accident problem, and to suggest effective ways to confront it.

From a conceptual point of view, our work has attempted to say something general about the nature, distribution and consequences of accident risks. From a practical point of view, it has aspired to specify the extent to which safety is (and could, or should, be) a social value, and to assess the relevance of local knowledge as a basis for public policy. A case study of the type we have completed is obviously only the starting point in taking these kinds of ideas forward. However, we believe that the experiences we have studied challenge the received wisdom sufficiently to enable us to argue that 'bottom-up' views of the distribution of risk and of the possibilities for prevention should be taken much more seriously.

Accidents as a problem

How problems are recognized and defined has a crucial bearing on how policies are shaped (Manning 1987), and the character of a policy instrument determines what that initiative can and cannot do to solve problems (Smith 1993). Child accidents are clearly a problem, and one which, given their frequency, distribution and effects, must merit governmental as well as parental concern. While illnesses such as diphtheria, whooping cough, measles and pneumonia, which at the turn of the century were major causes of child death in the UK, have retreated markedly over the past 80–90 years, mortality from children's accidents has fallen much more slowly. Moreover, children's accidents, which exhibit an unusually steep social class gradient in Britain, provide a salutary reminder of the extent and entrenchment of health inequalities.

The steep social class gradient in child deaths from accidental causes was one of the factors that brought us to this study. First, we were astonished that something so costly in children's lives, and so unevenly spread, should play such a minor role in the public health agenda. Since there are some societies where there is a much less marked social class difference in child accident deaths (and where the child accident rate overall is much lower), there is no need or excuse in other societies for retaining a situation where some children are more at risk than others simply because of the social status of their parents. There is nothing inevitable about inequalities in accident risks.

Second, we were concerned that, in the face of what appears to be an astonishingly marked and persistent health inequality, ideas about what causes accidents, and therefore suggestions on what to do to prevent them, have been subject to very little scrutiny or debate. As Jeanette Mitchell (1984) points out, one of the things we know when we look at a social class gradient in relation to an illness or death is that things do not have to be the way they are. If there are protective factors that prevent a social class I child from dying in an accident, these protective factors should be identifiable and, once identified, capable of being generalized to children from other backgrounds. The key questions, then, are how to identify the strategies that keep children safe and how to make these into accident prevention policies. The answer, in our view, depends partly on recognizing just what the problem of child accidents is.

In conceptualizing the problem of child accidents for policy purposes, there are two dominant views. Each carries a different policy prescription, so it is crucial when formulating accident prevention policies to be clear on which is the more plausible. *One idea is that child accidents are a consequence of poor people making poor parents.* Although usually masked by euphemism, the clear suggestion here is that parents in social class V, or parents whose social class is unclassified because there is no male wage earner in the household, either are not as aware or well educated about risks and dangers as parents in social class I, or are not as careful of their children. Additionally, a variety of psychosocial factors may mean that children of poorer parents are more accident-prone than average; they may be less predictable in their behaviour (Bijur *et al.* 1986, 1988b); and their parents may be less willing or able to supervise them closely.

If this set of explanations were found to be plausible, it would be logical to assign the responsibility for child accidents to the individuals at risk, and to argue that reductions in accidents are best achieved through health education and general parenting education. The aim here would be to reduce accident risks generally, and to tackle inequalities in accident risk in particular, by ensuring that less privileged parents are in command of the same knowledge about safety and child development as their wealthier neighbours.

The second possibility is that poor children are in greater danger than more affluent children because the environments in which they grow up are intrinsically riskier. If this is the more plausible explanation, then there are two kinds of preventive measure that follow. The first would aim to make the environments that poor people live in less risky, by designing out the dangers routinely built into them. The second would draw on skills that adults and children acquire and exercise precisely because they live in unsafe environments in order to produce locally sensitive suggestions about how the major hazards might routinely be avoided.

It should be clear from what we have already written that our findings lead us to formulate the problem of child accidents as something related to environment rather than to attitude and inclination, to institutional rather than parental neglect, and to place-based learning needs rather than general educational deficiency. As Chapter 3 shows, parents' views matter. Parents who live in Corkerhill know that their own children are more likely than children in the wealthier parts of the city to encounter an accident risk, and they know that in the environment of Corkerhill risks are more likely to turn into accident events than in many of the better neighbourhoods in the city. Moreover, parents have some important ideas about how to tackle this, and these ideas form the basis of the discussion of accident prevention policy that follows.

Policy and practice

We never expected or designed our work to produce a practitioner's or policy-maker's guide to how to prevent accidents to children. But our experience in exploring child safety in Corkerhill does suggest some clear ways forward for professionals, for parents and for children seeking to reduce risks. It seems to us to be important to place these policy recommendations on the table, for at least two reasons.

First, hitherto, accident prevention has been a minority occupation, attracting resources far below the level one might expect for a problem that causes more child deaths per year than cancer. There is, indeed, something of a policy vacuum around child accident prevention, with the result that where policies exist they tend to be fragmented. Accident management practices, and in particular preventive practices, are uncoordinated and piecemeal. This may be due in part to the fact that, in the public domain at least, accidents are either no one's problem or everyone's. Cross-sectoral working in local authorities, while gaining some ground, is still fraught with difficulties. On a national level, inter-departmental collaboration is similarly uncoordinated. With no public body taking overall responsibility for accident prevention, the lack of progress in the area becomes more understandable, though not, of course, excusable.

Second, accident prevention has, in practice, usually meant injury prevention. That is, the success of accident prevention policy has, where it has been measured at all, been specified in terms of a reduction in injury and death. This of course is the acid test of its success. But although they are a serious and important problem, deaths, and even serious injuries, resulting from accidents are thinly spread. This means that any reduction in risk, through, for instance, safer transport or safer housing, will be slow to recoup the investment in terms of lives saved. But our work suggests that making a community a safer place for children should have other effects on the quality of life and should make other gains in the area of public health and family life. As Chapter 5 shows, such changes could, for instance, lead to an improvement in the quality of life for families, a drop in maternal stress and an overall upgrading of local living environments.

From what has been said in the book so far, it is clear that successful accident prevention policies need to tackle two kinds of problem. First, such policies need to tackle the fact that, overall, the risks children face from accidents remain much higher than the risks they face from serious infectious diseases. For some reason, accidents have not been a marked part of the epidemiological transition that has otherwise substantially improved a child's chance of surviving to adulthood. There is, then, a general problem of higher than expected accident rates across the board. Second, accident prevention policy must be sensitive to the fact that while all health inequalities exhibit a social class gradient, the socio-economic gradient for child accident risk is more marked than any other. While we have explicitly avoided entering the complex (and often obfuscatory) debate on the causes of health inequalities generally, we would argue that for accident risks a large part of this inequality can be tackled through public policy and properly resourced community-based initiatives.

The management of child accidents requires, in short, both a strategy to reduce the overall accident rate and a strategy to prevent children from some class backgrounds, living in certain kinds of neighbourhood, facing significantly greater risks than others. In recent years, the emphasis has been placed very squarely on the first of these sets of strategies. Britain has, for instance, seen the introduction of flame-proof nightwear, child-resistant containers for poisons, safety belts for cars and similar innovations whose beneficial effects have been monitored and appear to be both dramatic and lasting. Child safety restraints, for instance, dramatically reduce risks to children (Agran et al. 1987; Christian and Bullimore 1989), as do cycle helmets (Thompson et al. 1989; Vulcan et al. 1992), though here there is some debate about the relative importance of the helmets themselves and the safe riding habits of helmet-wearers (Spaite et al. 1991).

In addition to these product-targeted safety measures, a range of public health initiatives has recently been introduced to deal with the overall child accident rate. These are part of a wider attempt to set national targets for health in the context of a far-reaching restructuring of the health services. This restructuring marks a shift in the nature of health interventions from cure to prevention, and it hinges on spreading the responsibility for public health away from the formal health services towards a variety of other statutory, voluntary and charitable bodies. In the government White Paper *The Health of the Nation* (HMSO 1992) national targets for accident reduction were set in the hope of: (a) reducing the death rate for accidents among children aged under 15 by at least 33 per cent by 2005 (from 6.7 per 100,000 in 1990 to no more than 4.5 per 100,000); and (b) reducing the death rate for accidents among young people aged 15–24 by at least 25 per cent by 2005 (from 23.2 per 100,000 in 1990 to no more than 17.4 per 100,000). The means to this end are the building of health alliances, the education of parents and children and the development of safety behaviours.

The NHS Management Executive in *First Steps for the NHS* (Department of Health 1992) has gone further, to set out some intermediate aims as a way of working towards these targets. These include reducing the incidence of accidents (primary prevention), reducing the severity of accidents (secondary prevention), improving the treatment of individuals who have suffered an accident, with a view to reducing mortality, resulting impairment or disability, and (tertiary prevention) improving care and support for those with disability resulting from accidents in order to minimize handicap.

The second, third and fourth aims, by and large, fall within the remit of one government department, the Department of Health, and one part of that department, the NHS. Responsibilities for the first aim (which by any standards must be the key aim) are less clear-cut. *First Steps* recognizes that attempts to lessen the exposure of children to risk by reducing the number of dangerous places, events and things to which they are exposed, to prevent dangerous events resulting in injury and to prevent minor accidents becoming major accidents is a multidisciplinary problem, but in suggesting ways forward the document is stronger on management rhetoric than on practical ideas. While the inclusion of 'action on accidents' as a key objective for regional and district health authority corporate contracts may be a welcome statement of intent, it does little to take us further forward. The suggested requirement that health promotion material relating to accident prevention be available in accident and emergency departments, community-based clinics and other appropriate locations and where appropriate be available in languages other than English, is sadly out of line with what (relatively little) is known about effectiveness. Certainly, the implications of our own work are not only that 'health promotion material' is very often irrelevant, since knowledge levels are high, but that such material is considered an affront by the people it is ostensibly designed to help.

Notwithstanding the high profile of education and information campaigns, what few investigations there have been of the impact of health education initiatives with respect to accident prevention have drawn similar conclusions. The evidence that these prompt any significant change in behaviour is rather less than one might think (Schlesinger 1966; Gerber *et al.* 1977; Minchom *et al.* 1984). The results of those health education programmes in child safety which have been evaluated have generally been disappointing (Dershewitz and Williamson 1977). Often, any evaluation that does occur concentrates on inappropriate outcome measures: there is little point in knowing that every health visitor working for a certain area has put a leaflet into the hands of every mother of an under-five, and given them personalized advice, if we do not know whether the accident rate is reduced, increased or unchanged as a consequence. And even when evidence is produced to suggest that health education messages are translated into behaviours, the net result does not seem to be a reduction in risk (Roberts and Coggan 1994). Two before and after studies evaluating the 'Play it Safe' campaign on British television found no evidence of reduced hospital admissions or reduced use of accident and emergency departments after it (Williams and Sibert 1983; Naidoo 1984).

On the other hand, there are no studies other than our own which explore the possible negative effects of such campaigns for the extent and consequences of heightened parental anxiety. The generation of anxiety in otherwise healthy populations in the absence of any measurable health gain may be an undesirable consequence of vigorous and enthusiastic health education; and when evidence of the desirable outcome of an overall reduction in the accident rate is lacking, the value of the policy must be questioned. This is well illustrated in the example of child pedestrian accidents. The Swedish child safety expert Sandels (1975) has argued convincingly that young children cannot be adapted to the road traffic environment. Yet most educational schemes designed to reduce road traffic accidents attempt to adapt children to traffic, rather than segregate them from it or target the behaviour of drivers. Injury reductions have not resulted from such initiatives in Britain (Antaki et al. 1986), and the ethical implications of – as one of our community consultants put it – 'teaching children to swim in a pool full of alligators' remain unadvised by safety initiatives whose net result may be to give children inappropriate confidence in their ability to cross the road.

Some success has been achieved in reducing the overall accident rate, more by targeting particular hazards and changing them to make them safe than adapting people's behaviours in risky places. Much less attention, however, has been paid to dealing with the socio-economic gradient in accident risks; and where this has been tackled, the touchstone has again been health education. The root of the problem, imply most policy documents and many prevention campaigns, is parents' and children's limited knowledge about risks and their propensity to engage in potentially dangerous behaviours.

Our research in a high risk community questions this assumption. Our findings suggest that parents do know a lot about accident risks (perhaps more than their counterparts living in less dangerous neighbourhoods) and that their daily routines are more geared to safe-keeping than to risk-taking. This leads us to make the following observations and recommendations about how the accident problem could be tackled generally, but with particular benefits to high risk areas and so with particular relevance to the problem of ironing out accident inequalities.

First, *most accidents occur in hazardous environments.* Spatial and socio-economic disparities in accident rates are partly a reflection of spatial and socio-economic differences in the incidence of risky environments. Accident prevention needs, therefore, to be concerned as much about environmental change as about behaviour modification.

The risks parents helped us to identify include factors associated with the design of the estate, such as road layout, on-street parking, the location of waste disposal facilities and so on. They also include factors associated with the design of the different housing types on the estate, such as unguarded flat-topped roofs, ungated external stone stairways, verandas with low rail-ings and dangerous gaps. Parents also expressed concern about the internal design of their homes, such as the location of the kitchen *vis-à-vis* the front door and the living room; and they talked of hazardous fixtures and fittings – live sockets, easily opened windows and so on.

In discussing these risks, parents are not slow to accept the importance of their own role in helping their children avoid them. Indeed, they all too frequently blame themselves for the hazards their children encounter. A mother described a near accident, when her child had touched an electric plug where the safety socket had not been put back in: 'I am going to murder someone for leaving that cover off, and it was probably me who left it off, because I am usually the last person using it.' Another mother, whose child had an accident in the bathroom, said: 'The problem was negligence . . . I blame myself because I should have been more careful to make sure he couldn't get into the bathroom.' What the 'blaming' at an individual level fails to do is to take into account the context in which a particular event occurs. In the case of the near accident, it was almost Christmas, a busy time in any household. In other cases, children will be left momentarily or longer because looking after children is only one of the things the mother has to do. If she is washing or cooking, is the child safer with her, or safer on its own?

Of course, in one sense, if a risk has turned into an accident because a back is turned, concentration has lapsed or patience has run out, parents do fail in their responsibilities. While the public responsibility for children's accidents is dispersed, unclear and under-resourced, the private respon-sibility is clear. Children are looked after by their parents, usually by their mothers. If anything happens to them, there has been a failure in parental competence. But all parents – rich or poor, educated or not – are prone to such 'failures': life is about more than constant vigilance to protect children from a single set of hazards. Parents have other things to attend to. The point is that in some environments the consequences of 'failing' to manage accident risks are more far-reaching than in others. At the moment, a prob-lem with a great deal of campaigning, public health and other work on child accident prevention is that it fails to recognize this, with the result that its expectations of children and their carers are unrealistic.

In practice, Stone (1993) suggests, between a third and a half of all accidents may be preventable through specific engineering, environmental or legislative measures. If we adopt a strategy of creating an environment that assists rather than obstructs safety behaviour, accident prevention policies might be more successful. As a general principle, it could be argued that public health measures mediated through environmental engineering are more likely to be effective than those predicated solely on changes in the attitudes, knowledge and behaviour of individuals. This would mean that traditional health education is less cost-effective as a means of accident prevention than is environmental engineering, although in practice the policy agenda operates as if the reverse were true (Stone 1989).

Second, *parents living in particular environmental settings know a lot about these environments*: they are the experts in identifying local risks. After all, they do keep most of their children safe for most of the time. In an unsafe environment, where accident hazards are routinely a part of daily life, parents who have to negotiate them have a lot of ideas on how they might best be managed. Requests for soft surfacing in the playground, speed humps on the main road, safety gates on communal stairs and so on are made on the basis of experience and they all represent small financial demands on the public sector for potentially significant gains in the privacy of the home. It may not be possible or feasible to adopt every suggestion that parents make, but their proposals are often very low cost strategies, and it is clear from our study that accident prevention campaigns which are not based on local knowledge will be severely limited in their scope and effectiveness.

At the moment, many of the data on which those trying to prevent accidents rely are anything but local. They are based on national, or at best regional, data, usually pertaining to accidents that result in injuries. There are no records of child accidents, only of child injuries, and usually only of those injuries which result in death or hospital admission. Not surprisingly, since these data are collected by health service staff, they tend to be focused more on the consequences of the accident than on the accident itself. Still less will be known about the antecedents of the accident; that is, what was happening before and at the time of the accident.

As a minimum, those who want to prevent accidents need to devise ways of collecting data at a local community level. People who live in a particular community may become used to the risks and dangers in that community, and may even find ways of avoiding them, but on the whole they know what the risks are. They can describe the street crossing that is out of order. They can talk about the hole in the fence leading to the railway line. Children will describe their own worlds of risks and dangers: the big dog; the scary house they will cross a busy road to avoid; the drivers who don't stop, even when the green man is on. Rather than simply describing the injuries or deaths of those children who get 'caught' by the dangers, local data need to catalogue what the risks and dangers are from the perspective of people who live with them.

We have found levels of 'lay' knowledge about risks and dangers to be high, not only among the parents, other adults and teenagers we interviewed for the work described here, but also among Glaswegian children as young as seven who took part in another piece of work on the way to or from, or at, school (CAPT and Roberts 1993). The idea that accident knowledge is the province of 'experts' is a mistaken view. For instance, in our survey we asked: 'If you had to choose the most unsafe feature of Corkerhill, what would it be?' Only one person could think of nothing. In including dangerous and risky places, environments and behaviours as well as accidents resulting in injury in local data, we are suggesting that recording and learning from 'near misses' and averted accidents are important aspects of safety behaviour. This has been recognized in other high risk fields such as aviation and anaesthetics, and is one of the ways in which all of us learn.

Third, a study of households' daily routines suggests that *strategies for safe-keeping are more apparent than irresponsible risk-taking among parents*. These safety behaviours could usefully be built into locally sensitive accident prevention strategies to provide relevant safety information for new parents and new residents. Notably, prevention policies need to explore the ways in which safety behaviours are integrated with and played off against other essential household routines. Just as local people are well-placed to recognize local risks and dangers, they are also likely to have devised strategies to deal with some of these and they have a wealth of original ideas for dealing with others. Lay people are more knowledgeable, imaginative and cost-conscious than most policy-makers think.

If our starting point is not that parents are ignorant and need educating but rather that, for the most part, parents are very successful most of the time in preventing accidents, then future strategies for accident prevention might look rather different from the way they do now. We need to have a national accident prevention programme, but we also know that much of the activity in preventing accidents takes place at a local level. Locally based preventive projects could draw on lay expertise and develop it in order to formulate local accident prevention strategies. Because such strategies would draw on local knowledge about local risks and dangers they are more likely to succeed in bringing the accident rate down than are existing health education campaigns. They have the additional advantage of being more likely to reduce the extent of inequality in the social and spatial distribution of accident risks.

Children and society

In an era of healthy alliances, there remains considerable ambiguity about who is responsible for tackling the problem of child accidents. Is child safety a personal, private domestic issue, or is it a problem for the public domain? Why is it that some public health issues remain largely personal tragedies, while others become public outcries? Is it simply, as Walter Morrison, one of our community consultants, has said, that child accidents are not contagious?

In the design of accident prevention policies, both bottom-up and top-down approaches have something to recommend them, and realistically, if resources are to be put into a problem, it has to be identified and prioritized at the top. However, a problem with top-down approaches relating to children in the United Kingdom is the very low status of children. Children are not seen as a priority. We under-invest in children in general, and as a society we find it rather more congenial, and substantially less costly, to adapt children to problems than to eliminate or reduce the problem. All kinds of policy decisions have implications for children – not simply decisions within the remit of the Department for Education and Employment or the Department of Health, but decisions of the Department of Transport, the Department of the Environment, the Home Office and the Treasury. For instance, Towner and her colleagues show that a journey made by car is three times more likely to injure a pedestrian than a journey made by bus (Transport and Health Study Group 1991), and the removal of public transport subsidies in London was followed by an increase in road casualties. What accident prevention strategies currently lack is not only a dimension sensitive to children's needs, as defined by both the children themselves and the parents responsible for them, but also an alliance with those policy areas whose activities have potentially most effect on the overall accident rate.

At both a national and a local level, a requirement to secure child impact statements for any new expenditure might begin to create a climate where the adverse (or beneficial) effects of initiatives on children would be explicit. At the moment this seems a completely unthinkable request. When a new motorway was planned to run within metres of Corkerhill, carrying a large volume of traffic and cutting Corkerhill off from the area of parkland close by, local residents made sure at the public enquiry that no one could be in any doubt about the effects they believed the road would have on the health and welfare of their children. The low level of car ownership in Corkerhill means that residents are unlikely to benefit substantially from a new road, but are likely to feel the adverse effects of noise, pollution and increased exposure to accidents. Their representations were unsuccessful. But our question is, should it be the responsibility of residents to draw attention to these disbenefits? Or should it be a requirement of the local authority to ensure that the cost to children and their communities is spelled out?

We have already outlined some of the ways in which we believe the relatively marginal place occupied by children shapes, or fails to shape, the policies that should protect them, and ideas on how to improve the situation have recently been put forward by the All Party Parliamentary Group for Children (1993). The Institute of Child Health, for instance, suggested preventive measures through 'changes in public transport policy together with small scale local measures and modifications to individual behaviour.' The Health Education Authority, the Royal Society for the Prevention of Accidents and the National Voluntary Council for Children's Play all called for traffic calming schemes and a greater emphasis on public transport, and the Children's Head Injury Trust and the National Association of Parent Teacher Associations called for legislation to be considered requiring the provision of play areas for children within new housing developments (All Party Parliamentary Group for Children 1993: 8).

It is clear from our descriptions of Corkerhill, however, that the overriding factors affecting the health and well-being of children and families in the neighbourhood are the debilitating effects of the marginalization of people whose lives are marked by poor housing, poor social facilities and poor access to jobs. Glasgow, a vibrant city, wealthy in world terms, provides ample evidence to support the arguments put forward by those describing the effects of poverty and relative deprivation on the welfare of children and young people (Whitehead 1988; Wilkinson 1994). We wrote at the start of this book about the weighty child protection procedures intended to protect children from violent injuries and death in the private sphere of the home. Those whose duty it is to protect children have not expended the same interest or energy on dangers in the public sphere that children face through poor housing, poor playspaces and an environment that is generally hostile towards children. While the rhetoric of the social welfare world is 'empowerment', the preferred mode of operation continues to be individual or family based interventions, with a focus on putting right parental deficits.

The work described in this book, however, demonstrates a reservoir of unused or underused knowledge and skills in the lives of parents and children. It demonstrates, we believe conclusively, that an attempt to address the social class gradient in children's accidents through behavioural or educational methods is doomed to failure. Dangerous families and dangerous people have frequently borne the brunt of state concern. Dangerous environments and the successful way in which, for the most part, adults and children negotiate the dangers are now due for more serious attention from those with a responsibility to bring down the accident toll. In the private sphere, we now know that safety is a key social value. Whether this is the case in the public domain remains an open question.

Bibliography

Adams, J.G.U. (1985). *Risk and Freedom: the Record of Road Safety Regulation*. London Transport Publishing Projects, University College London.

Adams, J.G.U. (1988a). Risk homoeostasis and the purpose of safety regulation, *Ergonomics*, 31(4), 407–28.

Adams, J.G.U. (1988b). Evaluating the effectiveness of road safety measures, *Traffic Engineering and Control*, June, 344–52.

Agass, M., Mant, D., Fuller, A., Coulter, A. and Jones, L. (1990). Childhood accidents: a practice survey using general practitioners' records and parental reports, *British Journal of General Practice*, 40(334), 202–5.

Agran, P., Dunkle, D. and Winn, D. (1987). Effects of legislation on motor vehicle injuries to children, *American Journal of Diseases in Childhood*, 141, 959.

All Party Parliamentary Group for Children (1993). *A Message to Parliament Concerning Children*. London, National Children's Bureau.

Alwash, R. and McCarthy, M. (1988a). Accidents in the home among children under 5: ethnic differences or social disadvantage?, *British Medical Journal*, 296, 1450.

Alwash, R. and McCarthy, M. (1988b). Measuring severity of injuries to children from home accidents, *Archives of Diseases in Childhood*, 63(6), 635–8.

Ampofo-Boateng, K. and Thomson, J.A. (1989). Child pedestrian accidents: a case for preventive medicine, *Health Education Research*, 5, 265–74.

Antaki, C., Morris, P. and Flude, B. (1986). The effectiveness of the Tufty Club in road safety education, *British Journal of Educational Psychology*, 56, 363.

Ashton, J. (ed.) (1994). *The Epidemiological Imagination*. Buckingham, Open University Press.

Avery, J., Vaudin, J.N., Fletcher, J.L. and Watson, J.M. (1990). Geographical and social variations in mortality due to childhood accidents in England and Wales 1975–1984, *Public Health*, 104(3), 171–82.

Avery, J. and Jackson, R. (1993). *Children and Their Accidents*. London, Edward Arnold.

Backett, E.M. and Johnson, A.M. (1959). Social patterns of road accidents to children: some characteristics of vulnerable families, *British Medical Journal*, 1, 409–13.

Bijur, P., Stewart-Brown, S. and Butler, N. (1986). Child behaviour and accidental injury in 11,966 pre-school children, *American Journal of Diseases in Childhood*, 140, 587–92.

Bijur, P., Golding, J. and Kurzon, M. (1988a). Childhood accidents, family size and birth order, *Social Science and Medicine*, 26(8), 839–43.

Bijur, P., Golding, J., Haslum, M. and Kurzon, M. (1988b). Behavioural predictors of injury in school-age children, *American Journal of Diseases in Childhood*, 142, 12, 1307–12.

Bjaras, G. (1987). Experiences in local community activities in Sweden: the Sollentuna project. In *Proceedings of the Healthy Community: Child Safety as a Part of Health Promotion Activities Conference*, Stockholm, April.

Bjaras, G. (1989). Organisations involved in a community intervention programme in accidents: local experiences in Stockholm County. Paper presented at the *First World Conference of Accident and Injury Prevention*, Stockholm, 17–20 September.

Bjaras, G., Danielsson, K., Schelp, L., Sjoberg, D. and Skonberg, G. (1990). Safety rounds in public environments: experience of a new tool for prevention of accidental injuries, *Accident Analysis and Prevention*, 22(3), 223–8.

Bjaras, G., Haglund, B.J.A. and Rifkin, S.B. (1991). A new approach to community participation assessment, *Health Promotion International*, 6(3), 199–206.

Blondel, B., Kaminski, M. and Rumeau-Rauquette, C. (1985). Mortalité des enfants de 1 à 4 ans dans les pays de la Communité Europeene', *Arch. Fr. Pediatr.*, 42, 645–9.

Blume, S. (1982). Explanation and social policy: the problem of social inequalities in health, *Journal of Social Policy*, 11(1), 7–31.

Brink, J.D., Imbus, C. and Woo-Sam, J. (1980). Physical recovery after severe closed head trauma in children and adolescents, *Journal of Paediatrics*, 97, 721–7.

Brown, G. and Davidson, S. (1978). Social class, psychiatric disorder of mother and accidents to children, *Lancet*, i, 378–80.

Brown, G. and Harris, T. (1978). *Social Origins of Depression*. London, Tavistock.

Brown, P. (1989). Popular epidemiology. In P. Brown (ed.) *Perspectives in Medical Sociology*. Belmont, CA, Wadsworth.

Brown, P. (1990). Popular epidemiology: community response to toxic waste induced disease. In P. Konrad and R. Kern (eds) *The Sociology of Health and Illness: Critical Perspectives*. New York, St Martin's Press.

Bryce, C., Roberts, H. and Smith, S.J. (1992). It's not all fireguards and safety gates, *THS Health Summary*, April, 7–8.

Bryce, C., Roberts, H. and Smith, S.J. (1993). *Safety as a Social Value: a Community Study of Child Accidents*. Glasgow, Public Health Research Unit.

Burgess J., Limb, M. and Harrison, C.M. (1988). Exploring environmental values through the medium of small groups: 1. Theory and practice, *Environment and Planning D, Society and Space*, 20, 309–26.

Child Accident Prevention Trust (1986). *Child Safety and Housing*. London, Bedford Square Press.

Child Accident Prevention Trust (1989). *Basic Principles of Child Accident Prevention: a Guide to Action*. London, CAPT.

Child Accident Prevention Trust (1992). *The NHS and Social Costs of Children's Accidents*. London, CAPT.

Child Accident Prevention Trust and Roberts, H. (1993). *Practice Guidelines: A Safe School Is No Accident*. London, CAPT.

Christian, M. and Bullimore, D. (1989). Reduction in accident severity in rear seat passengers using restraints, *Injury*, 20(5), 262.

Colver, A., Hutchinson, P. and Judson, E. (1982). Promoting children's home safety, *British Medical Journal*, 285, 1177.

Colver, A. and Pearson, P. (1985). Safety in the home: how well are we doing?, *Health Visitor*, 58(2), 41–2.

Constantinides, P. (1988). Safe at home? Children's accidents and inequality, *Radical Community Medicine*, Spring, 31–4.

Constantinides, P. and Walker, G. (1986). *Child Accidents and Inequality in a London Borough. Report to the North East Thames Regional Health Authority.* London, LSHTM.

Consumer Safety Unit (1989, 1990, 1992). *Home and Leisure Accident Research* (the HASS/LASS reports). London, Department of Trade and Industry.

Cooper, D.M. (1993). *Child Abuse Revisited: Children, Society and Social Work.* Buckingham, Open University Press.

Cooper, S. (1987). Education for planners and designers. In R. Berfenstam, H. Jackson and B. Eriksson, B. (eds) *The Healthy Community: Child Safety as a Part of Health Promotion Activities.* Stockholm, Folksam.

Davison, C., Davey-Smith, G., Smith, G. and Frankel, S. (1991). Lay epidemiology and the prevention paradox, *Sociology of Health and Illness*, 13, 1–19.

Department of Health (1988). *Protecting Children: a Guide for Social Workers Undertaking a Comprehensive Assessment.* London, HMSO.

Department of Health (1991). *Working Together under the Children Act, 1989.* London, HMSO.

Department of Health (1992). *First Steps for the NHS: Recommendations of the Health of the Nation Focus Groups.* London, NHS Management Executive.

Department of Health and Social Security (1980). *Report of a Working Group on Inequalities in Health: the Black Report.* London, HMSO.

Department of Transport (1988). *Road Accidents Statistics: English Regions.* London, HMSO.

Department of Transport (1991a). *Road Accidents: Great Britain.* London, HMSO.

Department of Transport (1991b). *Highways Economics Note No. 1 (November).* London, Department of Transport.

Department of Transport/Royal Society for the Prevention of Accidents (1986). *Accident Investigation Manual* (two volumes). London, Department of Transport.

Dershewitz, R. and Williamson, J. (1977). Prevention of childhood household injuries: a controlled clinical trial, *American Journal of Public Health*, 67(12), 1148.

Donzelot, J. (1979). *The Policing of Families.* New York, Pantheon.

Dougherty, G., Pless, I.B. and Wilkins, R. (1990). Social class and the occurrence of traffic injuries and deaths in urban children, *Canadian Journal of Public Health*, 81(3), 204–9.

Downing, C. and Franklin, J. (1989). *An evaluation of two local infant restraint loan schemes.* Paper presented at the First World Conference on Accident and Injury Prevention, secondary conference on Child Accident Prevention, Stockholm.

Erdmann, T., Feldman, K., Rivara, F., Heimbach, M. and Wall, H. (1991). Tap water burn prevention: the effect of legislation, *Pediatrics*, 88(3), 572.

Forrest, R. and Murie, A. (1988). *Selling the Welfare State: the Privatisation of Public Housing.* London and New York, Routledge.

Gerber, D., Huber, O. and Limbourg, M. (1977). *Verkehrserziehung in Vorshualter.* Cologne, Woolters Nordhoff.

Gibbons, J. and Bell, C. (1994). Variation in operation of English child protection registers, *British Journal of Social Work*, 24, 701–14.

Gorman, R., Charney, E., Holtzman, N. and Roberts, K. (1985). A successful city-wide smoke detector giveaway program, *Pediatrics*, 75(1), 14.

Graham, H. (1976). Smoking in pregnancy, the attitude of expectant mothers, *Social Science and Medicine*, 10, 399–405.

Graham, H. (1983). Do her answers fit his questions? Women and the survey method. In E. Gamarnikov, D. Morgan, J. Purvis and D. Taylorson (eds) *The Public and the Private*. London, Heinemann.

Graham, H. (1984a). Surveying through stories. In C. Bell and H. Roberts (eds) *Social Researching, Politics, Problems, Practice*. London, Routledge and Kegan Paul.

Graham, H. (1984b). *Women, Health and the Family*. Brighton, Wheatsheaf.

Graham, H. (1987). Women's smoking and family health, *Social Science and Medicine*, 25(1), 47–56.

Graham, H. (1992). *Smoking among Working Class Mothers*. Coventry, Department of Applied Social Studies, University of Warwick.

Graham, H. (1994). *When Life's a Drag*. London, HMSO.

Guyer, B., Gallagher, S., Chang, B., Azzara, C., Cupples, L. and Colton, T. (1989). Prevention of childhood injuries: evaluation of the Statewide Childhood Injury Prevention Programme (SCIPP), *American Journal of Public Health*, 79(11), 1521.

Haddon, W., Klein, D. and Suchman, E.A. (1964). *Accident Research: Methods and Approaches*. New York, Harper and Row.

Hamilton, D., Jenkins, D., King, C., Macdonald, B. and Parlett, M. (eds) (1977). *Beyond the Numbers Game*. London, Macmillan.

Hammersley, M. (1992). *What's Wrong with Ethnography?* London, Routledge.

Health and Safety Executive (1993). *The Costs of Accidents at Work*. London, HMSO.

Hedges, A. (1985). Group interviewing. In R.Walker (ed.) *Applied Qualitative Research*. Aldershot, Gower.

Heiskanen, O. and Kaste, M. (1974). Late prognosis of severe brain injury in children, *Developmental Medicine and Child Neurology*, 16, 11–14.

Hillman, M., Adams, J.G.U. and Whitelegg, J. (1990). *One False Move . . . : a Study of Children's Independent Mobility*. London, Policy Studies Institute.

HMSO (1992). *The Health of the Nation*. London, HMSO.

Hunt, S. (1993a). Damp and mouldy housing: a holisitic approach. In R. Burridge and T. D. Ormandy (eds) *Unhealthy Housing: Research, Remedy and Reform*. London, E. and F.N. Spori.

Hunt, S. (1993b). The relationship between research and policy; translating knowledge into action. In J. K. Davis and M. P. Kelly (eds) *Healthy Cities: Research and Practice*. London, Routledge.

Information and Statistics Division (1993). *Scottish Health Statistics, 1993*. Edinburgh, Directorate of Information Services, the NHS in Scotland.

Jackson, R.H., Craft, A.W., Lawson, G.R., Beatties, A.B. and Sibert, J.R. (1983). Changing patterns of poisoning in children, *British Medical Journal*, 287, 1468.

Janssen, S. (1991). Road safety in urban districts: final results of accident studies in the Dutch demonstration projects of the 1970s, *Traffic Engineering and Control*, 32(6), 292–6.

Jensen, A.-M. and Saporiti, A. (1992). *Do Children Count? Childhood as a Social Phenomenon: a Statistical Compendium*, European Centre for Social Welfare Policy and Research (Reproduced as the March–April 1993 *Childstats*, National Children's Bureau, London).

Jones, D. (1990). Child casualties in road accidents. In *Road Accidents: Great Britain 1989. The Casualty Report*. London, Department of Transport.

Katcher, M. (1987). Prevention of tap water scald burns: evaluation of a multi-media injury control program, *American Journal of Public Health*, 77(9), 1195.

Kendrick, D. (1993). Prevention of pedestrian accidents, *Archives of Diseases in Childhood*, 68, 669–72.

Kendrick, D. (1994). Children's safety in the home: parents' possession and perceptions of the importance of safety equipment, *Public Health*, 108, 21–5.

Klang, M., Ansersson, R. and Lindqvist, K. (eds) (1992). *Safe Communities: the Application to Industrialised Countries*. Lindköping Collaborating Centre Occasional Papers No. 5, Special Issue. Report from a Seminar in Lindköping, 26–27 November 1990. Lindköping, Department of Community Medicine, University of Lindköping.

Laidman, P. (1987). The role of the health visitor in child accident prevention within the control of the family. In R. Berfenstam, H. Jackson and B. Eriksson (eds) *The Healthy Community: Child Safety as a Part of Health Promotion Activities*. Stockholm, Folksam.

Littlewood, J. (1987). Housing conditions as a factor in children's accidents. In R. Berfenstam, H. Jackson and B. Eriksson (eds) *The Healthy Community: Child Safety as a Part of Health Promotion Activities*. Stockholm, Folksam.

Littlewood, J. and Tinker, A. (1981). *Families in Flats*. London, HMSO.

Lowry, S. (1990). Accidents at home, *British Medical Journal*, 300, 104–5.

Lynam, D. and Harland, D. (1992). *Child pedestrian safety in the UK*. Paper presented to the Forum of European Road Safety Research Institutes (FERSI), October.

Macdonald, K.I. (1995). Comparative homicide and the proper aims of social work: a sceptical note, *British Journal of Social Work*, 25, 489–497.

McCabe, M. and Moore, H. (1990). Is national fire safety week a waste of time?, *Fire Prevention*, 232, 12.

Mackie, A., Ward, H. and Walker, R. (1988). *Urban Safety Project 2. Interim Results for Area Wide Schemes*. London, Department of Transport, TRRL.

Mackie, A., Ward, H. and Walker, R. (1990). *Urban Safety Project 3. Overall Evaluation of Area Wide Schemes*. London, Department of Transport, TRRL.

McLoughlin, E., Marchone, M., Hanger, L., German, P. and Baker, S. (1985). Smoke detector legislation: its effect on owner-occupied homes, *American Journal of Public Health*, 75(8), 858.

Manciaux, M. and Romer, C.J. (1991). *Accidents in Childhood and Adolescence: the Role of Research*. Geneva, World Health Organization.

Manning, N. (1987). What is a social problem? In M. Loney et al. (eds) *The State or the Market*. London, Sage/Open University.

Martin, C.J., Platt, S.D. and Hunt, S.M. (1987). Housing conditions and ill health, *British Medical Journal*, 294, 1125–7.

Minchom, P.E., Sibert, J.R., Newcombe, R.G. and Bowley, M.A. (1984). Does health education prevent childhood accidents?, *Postgraduate Medical Journal*, 60(702), 260–2.

Mitchell, J.C. (1983). Case and situation analysis, *Sociological Review*, 31, 187–211.

Mitchell, J. (1984). *What Is to Be Done about Illness and Health?* Harmondsworth, Penguin.

Morrison, W., Rice, C., Roberts, H. and Svanstrøm, L. (1992). *Corkerhill, Glasgow: Application to Become a Member of the Safe Community Network*. White Report 275, August. Sundyberg, Karolinska Institutet.

Naidoo, J. (1984). *Evaluation of the Play it Safe Campaign in Bristol*. London, Child Accident Prevention Trust.

O'Donnell, M.J. (1990). Safety and health in the construction industry (letter), *British Medical Journal*, 301, 1101.

Parton, N. (1985). *The Politics of Child Abuse*. Basingstoke, Macmillan.

Parton, N. (1991). *Governing the Family. Child Care, Child Protection and the State*. Basingstoke, Macmillan.

Pharaoh, P. and Alberman, E. (1990). Annual statistical review, *Archives of Diseases in Childhood*, 65, 147–51.

Pless, I.B., Peckham, C.S. and Power, C. (1989). Predicting traffic injuries in childhood: a cohort analysis, *Journal of Pediatrics*, 115(6), 932–8.

Popay, J. and Young, A. (eds) (1993). *Reducing Accidental Death and Injury in Children*. Manchester, Salford and Manchester Public Health Resource Centre.

Pritchard, C. (1992). Children's homicide as an indicator of effective child protection: a comparative study of western European statistics, *British Journal of Social Work*, 22, 663–84.

Pritchard, C. (1993). Re-analysing children's homicide and undetermined death rates as an indication of improved child protection. A reply to Creighton, *British Journal of Social Work*, 23, 645–52.

Quick, A. (1991). *Unequal Risks, Accidents and Social Policy*. London, Socialist Health Association.

Ranson, R. (1987). *Home Safety: the Challenge to Public Health*. Coventry, University of Warwick.

Ranson, R. (1990). Home safety: the challenge to public health, *Journal of Sociology and Social Welfare*, 17(1), 93–109.

RCEP (1989). *The Release of Genetically Engineered Organisms to the Environment*, Royal Commission on Environmental Protection, thirteenth report. London, HMSO.

Rice, C., Roberts, H., Smith, S.J. and Bryce, C. (1994). It's like teaching a child to swim in a pool full of alligators. In J. Popay and G. Williams (eds) *Researching the People's Health*. London, Routledge.

Rivara, F.P. and Howard, D. (1982). Parental knowledge of child development and injury risks, *Journal of Developmental Behavioural Paediatrics* 3(2), 103–105.

Roberts, H. (1989a). When caring is forever, *Scotland on Sunday*, 28 May.

Roberts, H. (1989b). Rising protest at damp problem, *Scotland on Sunday*, 11 June.

Roberts, H. (1991). Child protection – accident prevention: a community approach, *Health Visitor*, 64(7), 219–20.

Roberts, H. (1992a). Professionals' and parents' perceptions of accident and emergency use in a children's hospital, *The Sociological Review*, 40(1), 109–31.

Roberts, H. (1992b). Risky business, *Times Educational Supplement*, 25 September.

Roberts, H. (1992c). School safety, *Child Safety Review*, Autumn, 14.

Roberts, H. (1995). *Intervening to prevent accidents*. In B. Gillham and J. Thomson (eds) *Child Safety: Problem and Prevention from Pre-school to Adolescence*. London, Routledge.

Roberts, H., Bradby, H. and Kelly, T. (1992a). Safe schools are no accident, *Streetwise: Quarterly Bulletin for the National Association of Urban Studies*, Winter, 12–13.

Roberts, H., Smith, S.J. and Bryce, C. (1993). Prevention is better . . . , *Sociology of Health and Illness*, 15(4), 447–63.

Roberts, H., Smith, S.J. and Lloyd, M. (1992b). Safety as a social value: a community approach. In S. Scott, G. Williams, S. Platt and H. Thomas (eds) *Private Risks and Public Dangers*. Aldershot, Avebury Press.

Roberts, H., Smith, S.J. and Lloyd, M. (1991). *Safety as a Social Value*. Glasgow, Public Health Research Unit.

Roberts, I. (1993). Why have child pedestrian death rates fallen?, *British Medical Journal*, 306, 1737–9.

Roberts, I. and Coggan, C. (1994). Blaming children for child pedestrian injuries, *Social Science and Medicine*, 38(5), 749–53.

Sandels, S. (1975). *Children in Traffic*, revised edition. London, Paul Elek.

Schelp, L. (1987a). Experiences in local community activities in Sweden. In R. Berfenstam, H. Jackson and B. Eriksson (eds) *The Healthy Community: Child Safety as a Part of Health Promotion Activities*, Stockholm, Folksam.

Schelp, L. (1987b). Community intervention and changes in accident pattern in a rural Swedish municipality. In L. Schelp and L. Svanström (eds) *Community Intervention and Accidents: Epidemiology as a Basis for Evaluation of a Community Intervention Programme on Accidents*. Stockholm, Folksam.

Schelp, L. and Svanstrøm, L. (eds) (1987a). *Community Intervention and Accidents: Epidemiology as a Basis for Evaluation of a Community Intervention Programme on Accidents*. Stockholm, Folksam.

Schelp, L. and Svanstrøm, L. (1987b). A model for registration and mapping of accident cases in health care, *Scandinavian Journal of Primary Health Care*, 5(2), 91–9.

Schioldberg, P. (1976). *Children, Traffic and Traffic Training: an Analysis of a Children's Traffic Club*, Geilo, Norway, International Federation of Pedestrians.

Schlesinger, E.R. (1966). A controlled study of health education in accident prevention, *American Journal of Diseases in Childhood*, 3, 490.

Scottish Office (1989). *Must do Better. A Study of Child Pedestrian Accidents and Road Crossing Behaviour in Scotland*. Consultants' report by the MVA Consultancy. Edinburgh, Central Research Unit Papers.

Sibert, J. (1975). Stress in families of children who have ingested poisons, *British Medical Journal*, 3(5975), 87–9.

Sibert, J.R. and Newcombe, R.G. (1977). Accidental ingestion of poisons and child personality, *Postgraduate Medical Journal*, 53, 254–6.

Sinnott, R. and Jackson, H. (1990). *Developments in House and Home Safety*. Coventry, University of Warwick.

Smith, S.J. (1987). Fear of crime: beyond a geography of deviance, *Progress in Human Geography*, 11, 1–23.

Smith, S.J. (1989). Social relations, neighbourhood structure and the fear of crime in Britain. In D. J. Evans and D. T. Herbert (eds) *Geography of Crime*. London and New York, Routledge.

Smith, S.J. (1993). Residential segregation and the politics of racialisation. In M. Cross and M. Keith (eds) *Racism, the City and the State*. London and New York, Routledge.

Smith, S.J. and Roberts, H. (1991). Accident prevention and local knowledge, *THS Health Summary*, October, 5–6.

Snashall, D. (1990). Safety and health in the construction industry (editorial), *British Medical Journal*, 301, 563–4.

Søderqvist, I. (1987). Experiences in local community activities in Sweden. In

R. Berfenstam, H. Jackson and B. Eriksson (eds) *The Healthy Community: Child Safety as a Part of Health Promotion Activities*. Folksam, Stockholm.

Spaite, D., Murphy, M., Criss, E., Valenzuela, T. and Meislin, H. (1991). A prospective analysis of injury severity among helmeted and non-helmeted bicyclists involved in collisions with motor vehicles, *Journal of Trauma*, 31(4), 1510.

Stewart, A. (1990). Safety and health in the construction industry (letter), *British Medical Journal*, 301, 1101.

Stone, D.H. (1989). Upside down prevention, *Health Service Journal*, 99, 890–1.

Stone D.H. (1992). A suitable case for prevention?, *Scottish Medicine*, 12, 5.

Stone, D.H. (1993). *Costs and Benefits of Accident Prevention: a Selective Review of the Literature*. Glasgow, University of Glasgow Public Health Research Unit.

Stone, D.H. with Roberts, H.M. (1992). *Housing and Health* (video). Glasgow, Media Services, University of Glasgow.

Suchman, E.A. (1961). A conceptual analysis of the accident phenomenon, *Social Problems*, 8(3), 241–53.

Sunderland, R. (1984). Dying young in traffic, *Archives of Diseases in Childhood*, 59(8), 754–7.

Tertinger, D.A., Greene, B.F. and Lutzker, J.R. (1984). Home safety: development and validation of one component of an ecobehavioural treatment programme for abused and neglected children, *Journal of Applied Behavioural Analysis*, 17(2), 159–74.

Tesh, S.N. (1988). *Hidden Arguments: Political Ideology and Disease Prevention Policy*. New Brunswick, NJ, Rutgers University Press.

Thompson, J., Ampofo-Boateng, K., Pitcairn, T., Grieve, R., Lee, D. and Demetre, J. (1992). Behavioural group training of children to find safe routes to cross the road, *British Journal of Educational Psychology*, 62, 173.

Thompson, J., Fraser, E. and Howarth, C. (1985). Driver behaviour in the presence of child and adult pedestrians, *Ergonomics*, 28(10), 1469.

Thompson, R.S., Rivara, F.P. and Thompson, D.C. (1989). A case–control study of the effectiveness of bicycle safety helmets, *New England Journal of Medicine*, 320, 1361–7.

Thomson, J.A. (1991). *The Facts about Child Pedestrian Accidents*. London, Cassell.

Tillman, M. (1992). *A Study of the Longer Term Effects of the Urban Safety Project. The Case of Reading, Berkshire*. Newcastle upon-Tyne, MSC Transport Operations Research Group.

Towner, E., Dowswell, T. and Jarvis, S. (1993). *The Effectiveness of Health Promotion Interventions in the Prevention of Unintentional Childhood Injury: a Review of the Literature*. HEA Policy Review. London, HEA.

Townsend, P. and Davidson, N. (1982). *Inequalities in Health: the Black Report*. Harmondsworth, Penguin.

Townsend, P., Davidson, N. and Whitehead, M. (1988). *Inequalities in Health: the Black Report and the Health Divide*. Harmondsworth, Penguin.

Transport and Health Study Group (1991). *Health on the Move. Policies for Health Promoting Transport*. London, Public Health Alliance, TRRL.

Transport and Road Research Laboratory (1991). *Accident Costing Research*. LF 2047. Crowthorne, TRRL.

Tucker, A. (ed.) (1991). *Report on the First International Conference on Safe Communities*, Falköping, Sweden, 3–5 June.

University of Glasgow (1992). *A Safe School Is No Accident*. Video and worksheet, available from 20 Southpark Avenue, Glasgow G12.

Vulcan, A., Cameron, M. and Watson, W. (1992). Mandatory bicycle helmet use: experience in Victoria, Australia, *World Journal of Surgery*, 16, 389.

Wadsworth, J., Burnell, I., Taylor, B. and Butler, N. (1983). Family type and accidents in preschool children, *Journal of Epidemiology and Community Health*, 37, 100–4.

Walker, R. and Gardner, J. (1989). *Urban Safety Project: the Nelson Scheme*. London, Department of Transport, TRRL.

Walker, R. and McFetridge, M. (1989). *Urban Safety Project: the Bradford Scheme*. London, Department of Transport, TRRL.

Ward, H. (1991). *Preventing Road Accidents to Children: the Role of the NHS*. London, HEA.

Ward, H., Norrie, J., Sang, A. and Allsop, R. (1989a). *Urban Safety Project: the Reading Scheme*. London, Department of Transport, TRRL.

Ward, H., Norrie, J., Sang, A. and Allsop, R. (1989b). *Urban Safety Project: the Sheffield Scheme*. London, Department of Transport, TRRL.

Ward, H., Norrie, J., Sang, A. and Allsop, R. (1989c). *Urban Safety Project: the Bristol Scheme*. London, Department of Transport, TRRL.

Webne, S., Kaplan, B. and Shaw, M. (1989). Pediatric burn prevention: an evaluation of the efficacy of a strategy to reduce tap water temperature in a population at risk from scalds, *Developmental and Behavioral Pediatrics*, 10(4), 187.

Whitehead, M. (1988). *The Health Divide*. Harmondsworth, Penguin.

Wilkinson, R. (1994). *Unfair Shares*. Ilford, Barnardos.

Williams, G. and Popay, J. (1994). *Researching the People's Health*. London, Routledge.

Williams, H. and Sibert, J. (1983). Untitled, *British Medical Journal*, 286, 1893.

Wilson, H. and Herbert, G.W. (1978). *Parents and Children in the Inner City*. London, Routledge.

Wise, P.H., Kotelchuck, M., Wilson, M.L. and Mills, M. (1985). Racial and socioeconomic disparities in childhood mortality in Boston, *New England Journal of Medicine*, 313(6), 360–6.

Wolfe, L. (1993). *Safe and Sound*. London, Hodder and Stoughton.

Woodroffe, C., Glickman, M., Barker, M. and Power, C. (1993). *Children, Teenagers and Health: The Key Data*. Buckingham, Open University Press.

Working Group on Inequalities in Health (1980). *The Black Report*. London, DHSS.

Wortel, E., Ooijendijk, W.T.M., de Geus, G.H. and Stompedissel, I. (1991). Volunteers as safety educators in a community campaign on child safety, *Health Promotion International*, 6(3), 173–80.

Wurtele, S.K., Gillispie, E.I., Currier, L.L. and Franklin, C.F. (1992). A comparison of teachers vs. parents as instructors of a personal safety programme for preschoolers, *Child Abuse and Neglect*, 16(1), 127–37.

Wurtele, S.K., Kast, L.C., Miller-Perrin, C.L. and Kondrick, P.A. (1989). Comparison of programmes for teaching personal safety skills to preschoolers, *Journal of Consulting and Clinical Psychology*, 57(4), 505–11.

Zelizer, V.A. (1986). *Pricing the Priceless Child*. New York, Basic Books.

Index

Page numbers in italic indicate reference to a figure or table. Page numbers in bold indicate a main section on a particular subject.